Learn Swift on the Mac

For OS X and iOS

DISCARD

Waqar Malik

Apress®

Learn Swift on the Mac: For OS X and iOS

Copyright © 2015 by Waqar Malik

ISBN-13 (pbk): 978-1-4842-0377-4

ISBN-13 (electronic): 978-1-4842-0376-7

Managing Director: Welmoed Spahr
Lead Editor: Michelle Lowman
Technical Reviewer: Ron Natalie
Editorial Board: Steve Anglin, Mark Beckner, Gary Cornell, Louise Corrigan, James DeWolf, Jonathan Gennick, Robert Hutchinson, Michelle Lowman, James Markham, Matthew Moodie, Jeffrey Pepper, Douglas Pundick, Ben Renow-Clarke, Gwenan Spearing, Matt Wade, Steve Weiss
Coordinating Editor: Kevin Walter
Copy Editor: Sharon Terdeman
Compositor: SPi Global
Indexer: SPi Global
Artist: SPi Global
Cover Designer: Michelle Lowman

Distributed to the book trade worldwide by Springer Science+Business Media New York, 233 Spring Street, 6th Floor, New York, NY 10013. Phone 1-800-SPRINGER, fax (201) 348-4505, e-mail orders-ny@springer-sbm.com, or visit www.springeronline.com. Apress Media, LLC is a California LLC and the sole member (owner) is Springer Science + Business Media Finance Inc (SSBM Finance Inc). SSBM Finance Inc is a Delaware corporation.

For information on translations, please e-mail rights@apress.com, or visit www.apress.com.

Apress and friends of ED books may be purchased in bulk for academic, corporate, or promotional use. eBook versions and licenses are also available for most titles. For more information, reference our Special Bulk Sales–eBook Licensing web page at www.apress.com/bulk-sales.

Any source code or other supplementary material referenced by the author in this text is available to readers at www.apress.com. For detailed information about how to locate your book's source code, go to www.apress.com/source-code/.

For my family, Irrum, Adam, and Mishal.

Contents at a Glance

Contents

About the Author

Waqar Malik worked at Apple helping developers write Cocoa applications for the Mac during the early days of Mac OS X. Now he develops applications for iOS and OS X in Silicon Valley. He is the co-author of *Learn Objective-C*.

About the Technical Reviewer

Ron Natalie has 35 years experience developing large-scale applications in C, Objective-C, and C++ on Unix, OS X, and Windows.

He has a degree in electrical engineering from Johns Hopkins University and has taught professional courses in programming, network design, and computer security.

He and his wife Margy split their time between Virginia and North Carolina.

Acknowledgments

I'd like to give thanks to all the folks at Apress who helped complete this book. This book would not have been possible without their assistance.

Introduction

Whenever developers come to a new platform, they are faced with the task of getting to know unfamiliar development tools, design patterns, the standard frameworks available in the new environment, and perhaps even a new programming language.

Most of the time, this is all done while trying to deliver an application as soon as possible. In such situations, developers tend to fall back on the patterns and approaches they are familiar with from previous environments, which too often results in code that doesn't fit the new environment, or in duplicate code that might already be provided by the built-in frameworks. This can cause problems down the road or delays in delivery.

It would be great to have colleagues already familiar with the platform who could offer guidance to get you going in the right direction. Well, it's not always possible to have mentors to help you, and that's where this books steps in—to be your mentor.

The author of this book is a veteran of Apple's Developer Technical Services organization, and has answered countless questions from software engineers who are new to Apple technology. That experience results in a book that anticipates the most common misunderstandings and takes care to explain not only the how, but also the why of Apple's development platform.

For example, the conceptual basis provided in Chapter 4, "Introduction to Object-Oriented Programming," gives you the means to place the material that follows into a coherent picture, instead of just tossing you into a flurry of unfamiliar classes, methods, and techniques and hoping you'll somehow sort it all out with practice.

Learn Swift on the Mac provides a step-by-step guide that will help you acquire the skills you need to develop applications for iOS and OS X.

Chapter 1

Hello Swift

Swift is a new language designed by Apple for developing iOS and OS X applications. It takes the best parts of C and Objective-C and adapts them with modern features and patterns. Swift-compiled programs will run on iOS7 or newer and OS X 10.9 (Mavericks) or newer.

The two main goals for the language are compatibility with the Cocoa and Cocoa Touch frameworks, and safety, as you'll see in the upcoming chapters. If you've been using Objecive-C, especially the modern syntax, Swift will feel familiar.

But Swift's syntax is actually a major departure from Objective-C. It takes lots of cues from programming languages like Haskell, C#, Ruby, and Python.

Some of the technologies I'll cover in this book are:

- Automatic reference counting
- Closures (blocks)
- Collection literals
- Modules
- Frameworks
- Objective-C runtime
- Generics
- Operator overloading
- Tuples
- Namespaces

Improvements over Objective-C

Let's take a quick look atsome of the features that make Swift better than Objective-C. I'll cover these in detail in later chapters.

Type Inference

In Swift, there is usually no need to specify the type of variables (though you can always specify them); the types of the variables can be inferred by the value being set.

Type Safety

Conversion between types is done explicitly. The compiler knows more about types in method calls and can use table look-up for methods for dispatch instead of the dynamic dispatch that Objective-C uses. Static dispatch via table look-up enables more checks at compile time, even in the playground. As soon as you enter an expression in the playground, the compiler evaluates it and lets you know of any possible issues with the statement; you can't run your program until you fix those issues. Here are some features that enhance safety:

- Variables and constants are always initialized
- Array bounds are always checked.
- Raw C pointers are not readily available.
- Assignments do not return values.
- Overflows are trapped as runtime errors.

Control Flow

The switch statement has undergone a major overhaul. Now it can select based not only integers, but also on strings, floats, ranges of items, expressions, enums, and so forth. Moreover, there's no implicit fall-through between case statements.

Optionals

Variables can now have optional values. What does that mean? It means a variable will either be nil or it will have a valid value. The nil value is distinct from any valid value. Optionals can also be chained together to protect against errors and exceptions.

Strings

Strings in Swift are much easier to work with, with a clear, simple syntax. You can concatenate strings using the += operator. The mutability of the strings is defined by the language, not the `String` object. You declare a string as either mutable or nonmutable with the same `String` object, by using either the `let` or `var` keywords.

Unicode

Unicode is supported at the core: You can define variables names and function names using full Unicode. The String and Character types are also fully Unicode-compliant and support various encodings, such as UTF-8, UTF-16, and 21-bit Unicode scalers.

Other Improvements

- Header files are no longer required.

- Functions are full-fledged objects; they can be passed as arguments and returned from other fuctions. Functions can be scoped similarly to instance variables.

- Comments can be nested.

- There are separate operators for assignment (=) and comparison (==), and there's even an identity operator (===) for checking whether two data elements refer to same object.

- There is no defined entry point for programs such as main.

If all this sounds good to you (it does to me), let's go get the tools to start playing with Swift.

Requirements

Before you can begin playing with Swift, you need to download and install Xcode, the IDE that's used to build applications for iOS and OS X. You'll need Xcode 6.1 or later.

It's really easy to download and install Xcode. Here are the basic requirements:

- Intel-based Macintosh computer

- OS X 10.10 Yosemite (or later)

- Free disk space

- An Internet connection

- An iOS device running iOS 7 (or later)

> **Note**   As a rule, the later the version of the OS, the better. The examples in the book are developed using Xcode 6.1 running on OS X 10.10 Yosemite and for iOS 8 running on iPhone 5S.

Getting Xcode

Launch the App Store application and use the search bar on the top right to search for Xcode. . You can then get more information by selecting Xcode, as shown in Figure 1-1, or install it by selecting the Install button.

Figure 1-1. Xcode on App Store

When you launch Xcode for first time, it will download and install other required items in order to complete the installation. If you have mutltiple versions of Xcode installed, be sure to select Xcode version 6.1 or later for the command-line tools. You can do this by selecting **Xcode ➤ Preferences**, then choosing the **Locations** tab as shown in Figure 1-2.

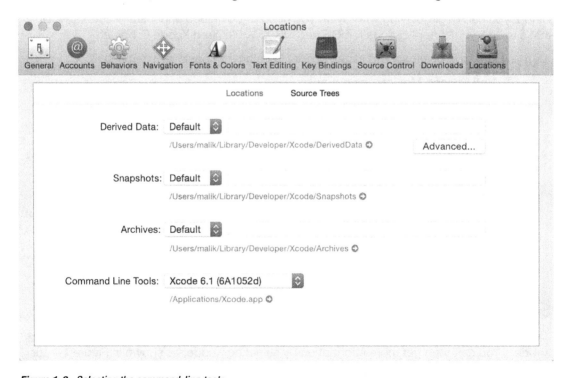

Figure 1-2. Selecting the command-line tools

Quick Tour of Xcode

If you launch Xcode without opening a project, you'll see the screen shown in Figure 1-3. You can create or open existing projects or a playground.

Figure 1-3. Xcode Welcome Screen

Let's start by creating a new playground, using the **Get started with a playground** option. As Figure 1-4 shows, the next screen asks you to name your playground and pick the operating system framework you'd like the playground to use. For now, just pick the default iOS and name your playground Learn Swift, then select Next to save your playground on your computer.

Choose options for your new file:

Name   Learn Swift

Platform: iOS

Cancel   Previous   Next

Figure 1-4. Naming a playground

And now you're ready to play with Swift. As you can see in Figure 1-5, line numbers are not on by default. To turn them on—and set all of your text editing preferences—select **Xcode ➤ Preferences** again and then select the Text Editing tab. The first option you'll see lets you enable line numbers, so you'll be able to easily find a line as I discuss it.

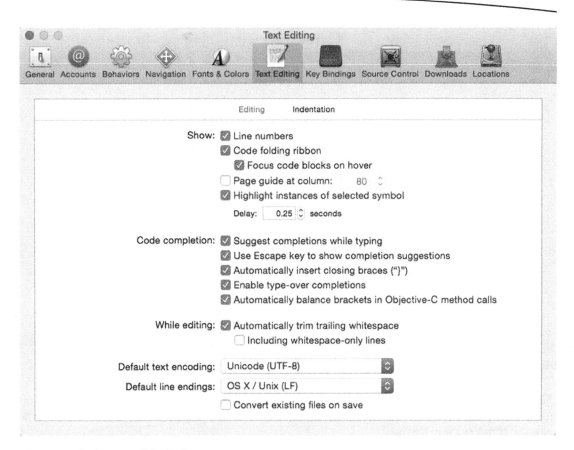

Figure 1-5. *Setting text-editing Preferences*

Once you have created the playground and updated the preferences. You will be greeted by the playground window as shown in Figure 1-6.

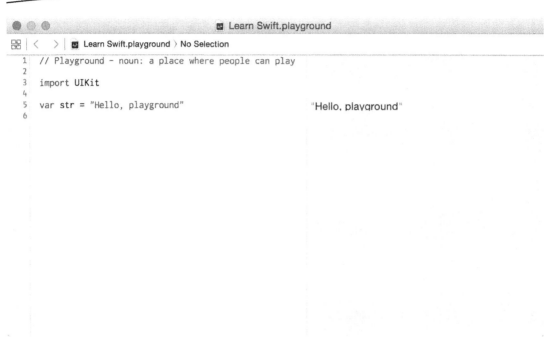

Figure 1-6. Interactive playground window

There are two parts to the playground. On the left, is the editor where you write code, and on the right is a sidebar that shows what happens when the code runs. As you can see, there is already some code in the file.

Line 1 shows a single-line comment, which starts with // and ends with new line. You can have as many as you like, but each must start on a new line. You can also use multiline comments, which start with /* and end with */ and can span multiple lines, like this:

```
/* this the first line of comment,
    it continues on the second line */
```

Line 3 tells the compiler to import the iOS Cocoa Touch API so I can use it if I want.

> **Note**   Cocoa is the framework that defines the API for developing OS X applications. Cocoa Touch is the equivalent for iOS. Sometimes Cocoa is used to mean both OS X and iOS and, in that case, the desktop version is referred to as AppKit.

Notice that there's no semicolon (;) at the end of the import statement, In Swift, semicolons are optional; they are required only if you put more that one statements on a line, such as var a = 4; var b = 8.

Line 5 is a variable declaration, which shows the keyword var and the name of the variable, and assigns the initial value to the variable. As you'd expect, the keyword var tells the compiler I'm declaring a variable. Then I give it a name; the default name is str but it could be any valid string (as I'll discuss in a later chapter).

Quick Tour of Swift

Whenever you learn a new language, there's a long-standing tradition that your first program is one that displays "Hello, World". Let's stick with that tradition. In Swift, this takes just one line:

```
println("Hello, Swift!")
```

This is a complete Swift program, so you don't need to import a separate library to use the function. And you don't need a special entry point, such as the main function in Objective-C.

Basic Types

To create values, you use either let or var. The first keyword, let, creates a constant value, which can be assigned only once; var creates a variable whose value can change during the execution.

```
var myVariable = 11
myVariable = 33
let someOtherVariable = 22
```

Notice that I didn't give explicit types to these variables. They are implicitly inferred from the type of value they were assigned, integers in this case.

If the type information can't be derived from the initial value, then it must be specified. You do this by adding the type specifier after the variable, separated by a colon (:)

```
var implicitDoubleValue = 1.0
var explicitDoubleValue : Double = 22
var a, b, c : Float
```

Values are never implicitly converted from one type to another type. Every type that needs to convert to anther type must provide a conversion function. Look at the following code:

```
var myString = "The answer is "
let answer = 42
let myAnswer = myString + answer
```

Swift would give an error here. You have to use one of the String functions that converts an integer to a string:

```
let myAnswer = myString + String(answer) + "."
```

What this does is create a new string from answer, which is then appended to myString and provides the final answer:

```
println(myAnswer)
```

Another way to insert values into strings is to use the \() expression conversion function To do this, you can write the expression:

```
let myAnswer = "The Answer is \(answer)."
```

The basic types are `String`, `Character`, `Int`, `UInt`, `Float`, and `Double`.

Aggregate Types

You can define arrays and dictionaries using bracket syntax.

```
var myArray : [String]()
var myDictionary : [String : String]()
```

The types within the brackets are the types of values aggregates can hold. Here I define the array to hold only string type values, and, for the dictionary, both the key and the value are of type `string`. But these don't have to be of type `string`; they can be `Int` or other aggragate types.

```
var myFavoriteFruits =["Oranges", "Bananas", "Grapes", "Mangos"]
myFavoriteFruits[2] = "Guavas"
var favorites = ["myFavorites" : myFavoriteFruits]
favorites["MishalsFavorite"] = ["Oranges", "Watermelon", "Grapes"]
favorites["AdamsFavorite"] = ["Apples", "Pears"]
```

Control Flow

You can choose `if` or `switch` for conditionals, and `for-in`, `for`, `while`, and `do-while` for loops. The paretheses around the contidional and loop variables are optional:

```
if a == b or if (a == b)
switch foo or switch (foo)
while a < b or while (a < b)
```

But the braces around the body are required:

```
If a == b
{
println("they are equal")
}
```

Functions

The syntax for a function is:

```
func functionName(arguments) -> returnType
{
}
```

or

```
func functionName(arguments)
{
}
```

In the second example, the function doesn't return a value.

> **Note**   You also use the keyword func when defining methods for classes.

Functions in Swift are full-fledged types. You can pass them as arguments and return them from functions. You can have a function that takes a function and returns a function. There's a special kind of function called a closure. Closures are unnamed functions that can be passed as data.You write the code for closures between {}:

```
{ (arguments) -> Int in /* body */ }
```

> **Note**   In Objective-C the concept equivalent to closures is blocks. When interfacing with
> Objective-C from Swift, blocks are imported as closures.

Objects

Use the keyword class to define class objects, similar to functions:

```
class MyClass {
}
```

Classes in Swift don't require parent classes.

```
class myClass : ParentClass, Protocol, AnotherProtocol
{
}
```

Use enum to create enumeration types

```
Enum : Int
{
  case One
  case Two
  case Three, Four, Five
}
```

The big difference in Swift for enums is they can include methods that operate on the cases of the enum.

Use the `struct` keyword to define structs:

```
struct MyStruct
{
}
```

Structs support most of what classes can do. But the big difference between classes and structs is that when passing structs around the code, they are always copies, while classes are passed by reference.

Generics

Generic types are used when you design a class that can operate on different types of objects, which allows maximum reusability of the code. You can have a linked list of integers or characters or strings. In a language like Objective-C, you'd end up using id or NSObject to hold different types of objects. In Swift, you define your object with a gerenic type in angle brackets <>. Then, anytime you have to define a variable with a method or somewhere in your class, you use the type that was given in angle brackets. Typically, developers use T for type, but when you instantiate the class you have to give a proper type, such as Int or Double or String.

```
class Node<T>
{
  var value : T
}

var myNode : Node<Int>
```

In this example T is replace with `Int`, and now Node can hold only `Int` type values.

Getting the Sample Code

Xcode is a large application and will take some time to download and install. While you're waiting, you can download the sample code for this book from the Apress site. Go to `http://www.apress.com/book/view/9781484203774`. In the middle of the page below the book description, you'll see a tab that says `Source Code/Downloads`, where you'll find the download link. Click that link to download the source code to your preferred folder.

Summary

You should have every thing you need now to start playing with Swift or developing your app. Don't forget to download the development tools and set up your development environment.

You've gotten just a quick overview of the Swift language so far. Next, we are going to jump right in and start to play with Swift itself. By the end of this book, you'l be writing programs yourself.

Chapter 2

The Swift Playground in Xcode 6

The Swift playground is a new interactive environment in which developers can view and manipulate their code live, instead of having to continually go throught the complete compile-run-test cycle. You type your code, it's evaluated, and you get feedback right away. You can see immediately whether your code is behaving as expected. Think of it as a mini project with one file and an SDK to compile against.

This chapter will walk you through creating your first playground and show you how to interact with the playground. You'll also create your first simple program in Swift. You'll be using playgrounds throughout this book, whenever you need to try out some standalone code.

I'll also delve into the different parts of the playground and discuss the functionality they provide, and show how to become really good at using playgounds.

Getting Started with a Playgorund

When you launch Xcode, you'll be greeted with its welcome screen, where you can create a new playground. If that window isn't visible, you can create a new playground by selecting **File ➤ New ➤ Playround...** or use **Option-Shift-Command-N** to get the dialog shown in Figure 2-1.

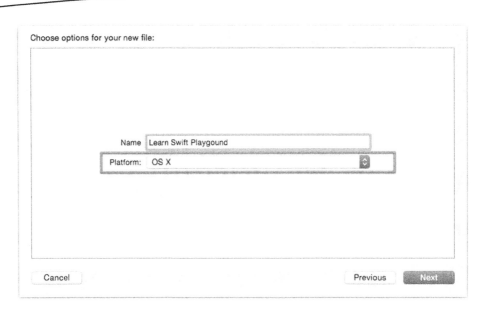

Figure 2-1. Naming your playground

Start by creating a new OS X playground, then name your playground and press Next. You'll be greeted by the window shown in Figure 2-2.

Figure 2-2. Playgound interaction window

There are two parts to the playground, the editor on the left and what's called the sidebar on the right. The editor area is where you enter code into the playground for Swift to interpret. The sidebar is where Swift will show the results and respond to your command if it has something to let you know. As you can see, there's already some code in the sidebar.

Line 1 is a single-line comment, as discussed in Chapter 1. Line 3 tells the compiler to import the entire desktop Cocoa API so it will be available for use.

Notice there's no semicolon (;) at the end of the import statement. This is because, in Swift, using semicolons to terminate a statement is optional if you only have one statement on a line. If you put more than one statement on a line, you must separate each statement with semicolons, except for the last statement. You can do this: var a = 4; var b = 8.

Line 5 defines a variable and then assigns a value to it. The default name is str, but it could be any valid string, (as I'll discuss in a later chapter).

You'll note that I didn't give the type of variable, such as Int or Float. That's because of type inference—Swift infers the type of the variable from the initial value assigned to it. Once the initial type is set for a variable, the type can't be changed. So, if you try to set an integer value to str, the compiler will give you an error, as line 6 in Figure 2-3 shows.

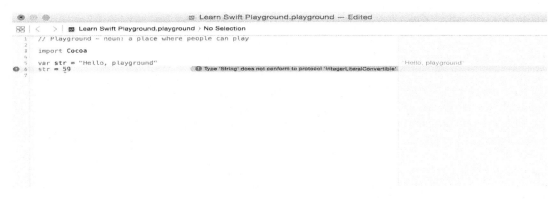

Figure 2-3. Error when the wrong type is assigned

This error says that the String type doesn't have a method that can take an integer argument and return a string when assigning to str.

Let's create another variable called value without assigning a value. The compiler is not happy, Because Swift is strongly typed, the language enforces the types for variables at compile time. If you make an error as you're writing code, you'll see the stop icon to the left of the line numbers. If you need to see the error message, click on the icon to display the error, as shown in Figure 2-4.

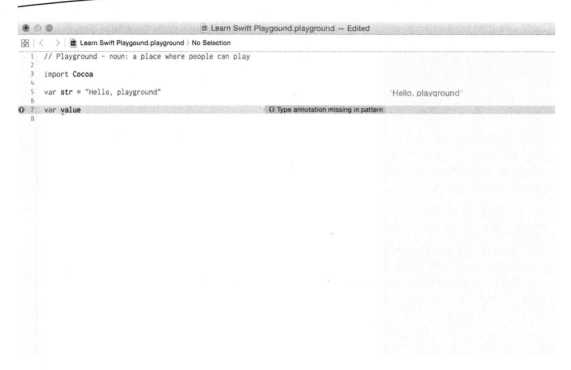

Figure 2-4. A missing-type error

To give a type to a variable in Swift, you add the type after the variable name, separated by a colon. If you write var value : String, the compiler is happy. However, if you try to use this variable in an expression, the compiler will again complain, because the variable has not yet been initialized, as Figure 2-5 shows. This is one of the Swift's safety requirements.

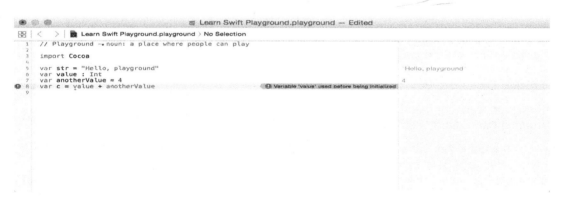

Figure 2-5. Uninitialized variable error

If you look at the right-hand side of the window—the sidebar—you'll see the result of the statement on line 5: the value of the variable str was set to the string "Hello, playground".

If you hover over the value on line 5, you'll see two icons on the right side of the line. The first, which looks like an eye, is QuickLook. Clicking it pops up a view of the object. The built-in types are supported and you can customize it for your own types. This is handy if the value is too long or complex to be displayed fully on the right side. The icon that looks like a circle brings up the value history display in the Assistant Editor.

To give this a try, type the following in the editor:

```
for i in 1...10 {
    i * i
}
```

Then select the value history and, as Figure 2-6 shows, the Assistant Editor will display a visual representation of the loop.

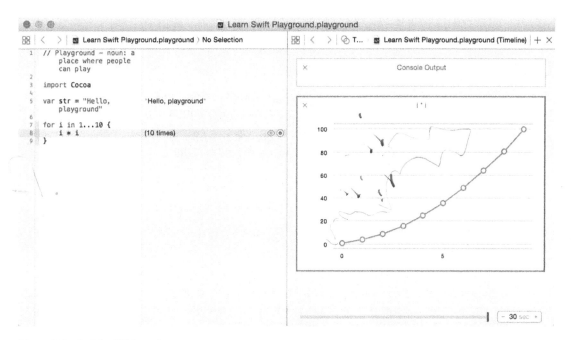

Figure 2-6. Assistant history view

The Assistant Editor uses QuickLook to visualize the output. The supported types are:

- Objects (Structs and Classes)
- Strings
- Images
- Colors
- Views
- Array and Dictionaries
- Points, Rects and Sizes
- Bezier Paths
- URLs (using WebView)

You can use use the `debugQuickLookObject` function to display objects that are derived from NSObject, which encompasses pretty much any existing Cocoa framework. Examples include UIImage, NSImage, UIColor, NSColor, UIView, NSView, and more.

Custom QuickLook Plugins

Because you're not yet familiar with the language, you might find the following examples a bit terse. Still, they will give you an idea how powerful playgrounds can be.

To develop a custom plugin, you use the XCPlayground module, which has three functions that let you display custom values and views in the Assistant Editor.

> **Note**   XCPlayground only works for NSView- and UIView-based subviews.

XCShowView

If you're developing a custom view and want to see how it's going, you can call this method to display what the view looks like. XCShowView takes an identifier that's displayed at the top of the view so you know which view is being displayed.

```
XCShowView(identifier : String, view : NSView)
XCShowView(identifier : String, view : UIView)
```

XCCaptureValue

If you're developing your program and want to display some values, you can use the XCCaptureValue function to display the values:

```
XCCaptureValue<T>(identifier : String, value : T)
```

XCPSetExecutionShouldContinueIndefinitely

Client/server communication is common in mobile computing, but the network is inherently unreliable. As a result, most communication is therefore asynchronus, where the client makes a call to server and when the server returns the response, the client then acts on it. But the call gets executed quickly and runs on the background thread. If the tasks on the main thread finish too quickly, the program could exit without giving the client a chance to process the response from the server. To prevent this, use the XCPSetExecutionShouldContinueIndefinitely function to keep the main program from terminating.

This function allows you to execute long-running asynchronous tasks. Here's how you could use it to download some JSON data from the network:

```
XCPSetExecutionShouldContinueIndefinitely(continueIndefinitely: Bool = default)
```

Custom Modules for Playground

These functions are all good, but suppose you have your own code and don't want to copy and paste it into the playground, you just want to use your own classes in the playground. This is possible, but there are some prerequisites:

- The code must be in a framework.
- The classes you plan to use in the playground must have public access.
- The playground must be in the same workspace as the project with the framework.
- The framework must already be built.
- For iOS, the framework must be built for a 64-bit runtime.
- There must be a scheme that builds a target.
- Build location preference must be set to Legacy.
- The playground name must not be same as the build target.

Importing Your Code

Once you've fulfilled these conditions, you can simply use `import ModuleName` to import your code into the playground.

Now let's start create a framework. Launch Xcode and select the **Create a new Xcode project** option, as shown in Figure 2-7.

Figure 2-7. Xcode Welcome window

On the next screen you'll be asked to select the template for the project, as shown in Figure 2-8. Under iOS, select **Framework & Library**, and then choose **Cocoa Touch Framework**.

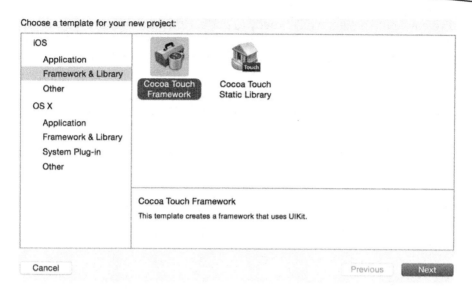

Figure 2-8. Framework template window

Next, give the framework a name and fill in other required information. Be sure to select **Swift** for the Language option.

Choose options for your new project:

Product Name:

Organization Name: Apress, Inc.

Organization Identifier: com.apress

Bundle Identifier: com.apress.ProductName

Language: Swift

Cancel   Previous   Next

Figure 2-9. Naming the framework and language selection

Once you've saved the project, you're ready to code. However, you also need a workspace, which is where you combine your frameworks and sources. To create a workspace from an existing open project, select the **File ➤ Save as Workspace...** option and give it the same name as the project.

Next you need to create some types for your framework that you'll use in the playgournd. Create a new file by selecting **File ➤ New ➤ File...**. Be sure to select **iOS ➤ Source ➤ Swift File**.

Note   You can also import your existing code to the framework.

Now enter the following code:

```
public class Chapter2
{
    var message : String
    public init(_ message : String)
    {
        self.message = message
    }

    public func printMessage()
    {
        println(message)
    }
}
```

Next you need to add an example project that has your framework as a dependency. Do this using **File ➤ New ➤ Target...**, choose **iOS ➤ Application ➤ Single View Application** (see Figure 2-10).

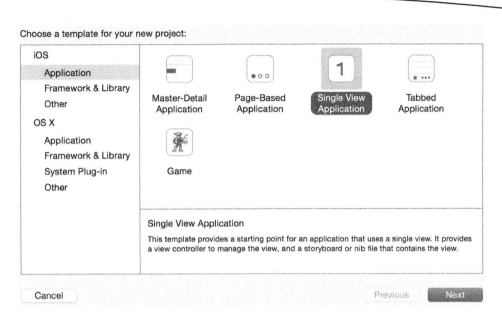

Figure 2-10. iOS Application Template window

Give the new application the name **Chapter2Example.** Now the app needs to depend on the framework. Select the project and then select **Chapter2Example** as the target. As you can see in Figure 2-11, one of the options is **Build Phases**, which is where you're going to add the dependency.

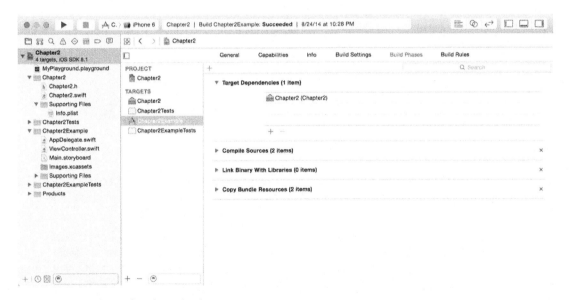

Figure 2-11. Setting project dependencies

Figure 2-12 shows the window where you choose the dependent framework.

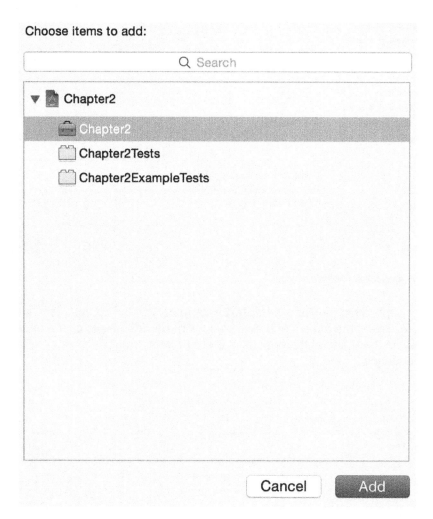

Figure 2-12. Dependent framework selection window

Now that we have the settings out of the way, now we need to build the application and test it. Select the Build option from the project menu or **Command-B**. This will build the application and in turn the framework because of the dependency setup.

Next you create a playground into which you'll import your framework and use the code that was defined in Framework. At the bottom left of the Xcode window, in the project navigator view, select the **+** button. This brings up a menu with options to add different items to the project, one of which is the new playground. Select this option and save the new playground. The new playground will be automatically added to the project workspace.

Now select the playground in the project navigator and insert the following code under the first import statement:

```
import Chapter2
var hello = Chapter2("Hello, framework")
hello.printMessage()
```

If you open the Assitant Editor, you'll see your output from the framework. Keep in mind that if you change any code in the framework, you'll need to build the application so that the framework gets rebuilt. If you don't do this, the new code won't be available in the playground.

Summary

You learned what Swift playgrounds are and how they can help you develop code visually. You saw how to create a framework, how to make your project depend on the framework, and how to import your framework into your playground. You can also share you playground just as you can share your projects.

Playgrounds are good for learning and doing quick prototyping your code, but they do have limitations:

- Playgrounds are not good for performance testing.
- You can't interact with views.
- Playgrounds can't run on mobile devices.

Chapter 3

Accessing Swift's Compiler and Interpreter: REPL

Let's now investigate how to access the Swift compiler from the command-line interface known as the **R**ead-**E**val-**P**rint-**L**oop, or REPL. This is where you can interact with the compiler by entering statements, which the compiler will interpret and evaluate immediately.

What is REPL?

The REPL is an interactive shell that's similar to the Unix shell and those of other languages like Lisp, Ruby, and Python. When you start the shell, you are given a prompt to enter your code. The compiler interprets and evaluates the code and then prints either the result or an error.

If you don't have Terminal in the Dock, locate the Terminal app in the Utilities folder and drag it to the Dock, then launch it by selecting it from the Dock.

With Terminal running, you access REPL by typing **swift** at the prompt. Assuming the command-line tools have been set up correctly, you'll then see the Swift welcome message, like this:

```
tardis:~ malik$ swift
Welcome to Swift!  Type :help for assistance.
  1>
```

If that doesn't work, try entering **xcrun swift**. If you still get an error, Swift is probably not set up correctly.

```
tardis:~ malik$ swift
swift: error: unable to find utility "swift", not a developer tool or in PATH
```

To fix this problem you can use a utility called xcode-select, which is installed when you install and run the Xcode tools. To test whether the command-line tools were installed correctly, use the following command to find which version of the command-line tools is being used:

```
tardis:~ malik$ sudo xcode-select --print-path
/Applications/Xcode.app/Contents/Developer
```

If you are running an older version of Xcode, or more that one version, you will want to select Xcode 6.1 or later for the command-line tools. You can do this from command line using the xcode-select command:

```
tardis:~ malik$ sudo xcode-select -switch /Applications/Xcode6.app.
```

You can also do it by going to **Xcode ➤ Preferences** and selecting the Locations tab, as shown in Figure 3-1.

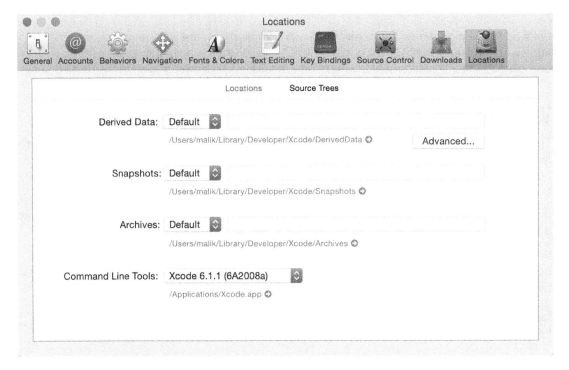

Figure 3-1. Selecting the Command Line Tools version

This will set the location of the command-line tools that are part of the Xcode6.app package.

Once you've set the paths correctly and are at the Swift prompt in the REPL, you can enter the code you want the compiler interpret. When you're finished playing with the REPL, just type **:quit** and you'll be back in your previous shell.

LLDB and the Swift REPL

You can also use the REPL in LLDB, which is the default debugger in Xcode. If you're running a program, you'll have to pause execution of that program to get to the debugger prompt. Once the program has stopped, either at a breakpoint in your program or because you selected the pause button in the debug window, just type **repl** to get the REPL.

```
(lldb) repl
>
```

To get back to LLDB just type a colon : and press Enter and you'll be back in the debugger.

```
  1> var a = "Hello"
a: String = "Hello"
  2> var b = "REPL"
b: String = "REPL"
  3> println(a +
  4. ", " + b)
Hello, REPL
  5>
```

You can also compile your program using the command-line compiler swiftc, or run your script using the Swift REPL.

```
swift hello.swift
```

There are quite a few options for the interpreter. Type **swift –help** to display the options and get help specific to the Swift application. The basic command structure is **swift [options] <inputs>** where [options] are any of the listed options. For example, if you wanted to link to a custom framework, you'd use the **–framework <name>** option.

When looking at these options, note that the values between the square brackets [ ] are optional and those between the angle brackets <> are required. You replace them, including the brackets, with your specific values. In the following example, I run the mylocation.swift source file and link to the CoreLocation.framework:

```
tardis:~ malik$ swift –framework CoreLocation.framework mylocation.swift
```

This example will not create an executable, it just interprets the statement. To compile the file and make it executeable, you'd use the Swift compiler, swiftc. Let's give it a try.

Create a file using your favorite editor and name it Hello.swift. Now add the following code:

```
println("Hello, Compiler")
```

This is a simple statement that prints a message. After you've added the code and saved the file, compile the file using the following command:

```
tardis:Chapter3 malik$ swiftc Hello.swift -o Hello
```

This command compiles Hello.swift and outputs an executeable—a standalone program called Hello. Now you can take this program and run it without the Swift interpter. That's the difference between an interpreter and a compiler. To the run the executable, you just type its name. If you get an error because your current path is not part of your PATH variable, just tell the interpreter that the file is located in the current directory by prepending ./ to the name of the execuable:

```
tardis:Chapter3 malik$ ./Hello
Hello, Compiler
```

Now add the following line of code, keeping in mind that once you've edited the file, you have to recompile it to recreate the executable with new code. If you don't, either you will not have an execuable or have an executable that was compiled with previous iteration of the code.

```
prinln("Hello, Again)
tardis:Chapter3 malik$ swiftc Hello.swift -o Hello
Hello.swift:5:1: error: use of unresolved identifier 'prinln'
prinln("Hello, Again")
^
```

Oh no, that doesn't look good. Can you guess what happened? Yes, that's correct. There's an error in the code. The compiler is kind enough to tell me where I've made the mistake.

First, it indicates that the error is in the Hello.swift file. In this case, that's the only file, but if you're compiling more than one file, this message is helpful. The next two numbers, :5:1:, are the row and column in the file where the error was triggered, followed by the actual error message from the compiler, indicating that it doesn't know the function prinln. Finally, the next two lines show the actual line of the code and a ^ where the error was triggered.

Yes, I misspelled the println function. I'll fix the error and try again.

```
println("Hello, Compiler")

println("Hello, Again")
swiftc Hello.swift -o Hello
tardis:Chapter3 malik$ ./Hello
Hello, Compiler
Hello, Again
```

Success! After I recompiled the file, everything worked as expected.

Summary

You learned how to set up the command-line tools so you can access both the Swift compiler and interpreter. You found out what REPL is and how Swift can be accessed from the Terminal app and the LLDB debugger using the REPL. Finally, you learned how to compile a swift file using the compiler to generate an executable program.

Chapter 4

Introduction to Object-Oriented Programming

If you have any experience with programing, chances are good you've at least heard the term *object-oriented programming*, OOP for short. This is one of the techniques used when programming, along with structured and functional programming.

OOP was developed for writing simulation programs, but because the benefits of the technique became readily apparent, it was soon adapted for writing general-purpose programs.

OOP is a way to construct objects that perform specialized tasks in tandem with other objects, by communicating with each other using defined interfaces. This chapter provides an overview of OOP's concepts and principles.

I'll be using some terms that require explanation, so before we move on, I'm going to define few of these.

- *Class* is a data structure that defines a type of object; it encompasses data and the functions that operate on that data.

- *Subclass*, *child class*, and *derived class* refer to a class that inherits from another class, including attributes such as variables and functions.

- *Superclass*, *parent class*, and *base class* refer to a class that other classes can inherit attributes from.

- *Instance* or *object* refer to the actual creation of a particular class.

- *Method* is a function associated with a particular class.

- *Interface* is a set of properties and methods that provide access to an object.

> **Note**   Object-oriented programming was first developed at the Norwegian Computer Center, which developed languages called Simula 1 and Simula 67. Simula 67 introduced the concepts of objects, classes, inheritance, and subclasses. Now we have modern languages like C++, Java, Objective-C and now Swift that build on those basic principles.

The Concept Behind OOP

The basic concept of OOP is indirection; instead of using variables directly, you provide an interface. Let's say you want to give a package to a friend. There are multiple ways to get that package to him or her.

- You can drive over to her house and drop off the package.

- You can have another friend drive to her house and drop off the package.

- You can simply mail the package.

The second and third items involve indirection—instead of you doing the work, you have someone else do the work for you.

This is a simple example, but you can take this indirection to multiple levels. Say you've been working for Super Mega Corp and you need to take your vacation. You talk to your manager, who talks to his manager and then to HR. Finally, you get word that your vacation is approved. When you ask your manager (an object, in this case) for approval, that's the interface, but that interface communicates with other objects to give you an answer.

Indirection and Variables

When you use a variable in your programs, you're using indirection. Take a look at this example program:

```
func counting1 () {
println("Integers from 1 to 5")
    for i in 1...5 {
        println(i)
    }
}

counting1()
```

This simple program will print integers from 1 to 5.

```
Integers from 1 to 5
1
2
3
4
5
```

Now suppose you want to print integers from 1 to 10, or to any number. You'll need to update the program at two places:

```
func counting2 () {
    println("Integers from 1 to 10")
    for i in 1...10 {
        println(i)
    }
}
```

This change was simple and straightforward because the function is pretty small, but imagine doing this in a program spanning multiple files with thousands of lines of code. If you simply did a search and replace, you might inadvertently change the wrong numbers or not change the correct ones.

To solve this problem, a better idea is to use the variable count to hold the upper limit for the loop. In this way I add indirection to the program. I then have to make a change in only one place and tell the program to count from 1 to whatever value the count variable holds.

```
func counting3 () {
    let count : Int = 5
    println("Integers from 1 to \(count)")
    for i in 1...count {
        println(i)
    }
}
```

I have to change just the value of the count variable in one place and it gets propagated. I can take indirection one step further and make the count an argument to the function to make it even more flexible.

```
func counting4 (count : Int) {
    println("Integers from 1 to \(count)")
    for i in 1...count {
        println(i)
    }
}
```

OOP uses indirection to the maximum level; you can say OOP is all about indirection. You just saw how to use indirection with data, but the real OOP revolution is the indirection related to *code*. Instead of calling a function directly, you might call that function indirectly.

Procedural Programming

Why jump in here and talk about procedural programming? To get the real benefits of OOP, you need to understand the problem it tries to solve. Procedural programming has been around for a long time and it's typically taught in beginning courses, using language like C, Pascal, or Perl.

In procedural programming the data is kept separate from the code, and that data is passed to each function to interpret and process. Because procedural programming is centered on functions, you have to decide which function to call and when.

Let's take a simple example in which the program draws different geometric shapes with different colors.

> **Note**   To keep the program simple, it won't actually draw shapes. Instead, it will just print a message that says it's drawing a shape.

First, I need to define a type for shape, so I'll define an enum called ShapeType:

```
enum ShapeType {
    case Circle
    case Triangle
    case Rectangle
}
```

Next I define the colors to use to fill the shapes:

```
enum ShapeColor {
    case Red
    case Blue
    case Green
}
```

I'll define the bounding box—the area where these shapes will be drawn:

```
struct ShapeRect {
    var x : Float
    var y : Float
    var width : Float
    var height : Float
}
```

With these three items defined, I can finally define the Shape structure, which has three elements, bounds, color and type.

```
struct Shape {
    var type : ShapeType
    var color : ShapeColor
    var bounds : ShapeRect
}
```

Next I'm going to define a function that creates three shapes, then calls another function to draw each shape.

```
func shapes () {
    var shapes = [Shape]()
    shapes.append(Shape(type: .Circle, color: .Red, bounds: ShapeRect(x: 0, y: 0,
    width: 10, height: 20)))
    shapes.append(Shape(type: .Rectangle, color: .Blue, bounds: ShapeRect(x: 30,
    y: 40, width: 50, height: 60)))
    shapes.append(Shape(type: .Triangle, color: .Green, bounds: ShapeRect(x:10,
    y: 20, width: 60, height: 80)))

    drawShapes(shapes)
}
```

The shapes function creates one shape for each of the types I've defined, and after creating the shapes array, the function calls the drawShapes function, which takes an array of shapes.

```
func drawShapes(shapes : [Shape])
{
    for shape in shapes {
        switch shape.type {
        case .Circle:
            drawCircle(shape)
        case .Rectangle:
            drawRectangle(shape)
        case .Triangle:
            drawTriangle(shape)
        }
    }
}
```

The drawShapes function will iterate over the array of shapes, find the type of each shape, and then call the appropriate draw function to draw the shape.

When you run this program you'll get the following output:

```
Drawing Circle
Drawing Rectangle
Drawing Triangle
```

You probably noticed that I spent most of the time passing the data around different functions. Connecting data with the proper functions can get tedious, and you can end up calling a function with the wrong data or vice versa.

Another big problem with procedural programming is that extending and maintaining the code can be difficult and time-consuming. To illustrate, I'm going to add a new shape to draw called Hexagon. I have to modify the program in various locations to do this:

- Add a new shape type to ShapeType.

- Add a new case for Hexagon to drawShapes.

- Add a drawHexagon function to draw the new shape.

If you skip any of these changes, you won't get the results you want. How will you miss any of these items? Well, this is a simple program, but imagine a complex program where you'd have to go through tons of code. And I didn't even address the issue of whether the new shape needed more data, in which case you'd have to extend the Shape object to add the necessary data.

Objected Oriented Implementation

You probably noticed that functions are the focus in procedural programming and data is passed around. In OOP, it's the opposite: you focus on the data and the functions get passed around. How is that different from procedural programming?

- In procedural programming, you tell the function drawRectangle to take the data and draw a rectangle.

- In OOP, you tell the shape rectangle (an object) to draw itself. The focus is on the object (rectangle).

So what is an object? It's a term that describes data and the functions that can operate on that data. In my example, each shape is an object.

Let's define classes for each of these objects.

> **Note** In Swift you use the keyword class to define an object.

```
class Circle {
      var color : ShapeColor
      var bounds : ShapeRect
       init (bounds : ShapeRect, color : ShapeColor) {
           self.bounds = bounds
           self.color = color
      }

  func draw () {
      println("Drawing Circle")
    }
}

class Rectangle {
    var color : ShapeColor
    var bounds : ShapeRect
    init (bounds : ShapeRect, color : ShapeColor) {
        self.bounds = bounds
self.color = color
    }

    func draw () {
        println("Drawing Rectangle")
    }
}
```

```
class Triangle {
var color : ShapeColor
    var bounds : ShapeRect
    init (bounds : ShapeRect, color : ShapeColor) {
        self.bounds = bounds
self.color = color
    }

    func draw () {
        println("Drawing Triangle")
    }
}
```

Now that I have the objects, I can change the drawShapes function to just iterate over the array and send a draw message to each object to draw itself, as shown here.

```
func drawShapes(shapes : [AnyObject])
{
    for shape in shapes {
        shape.draw()
    }
}
```

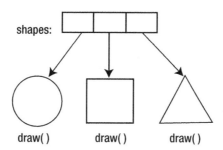

Now the code for this function is much simpler and I even got rid of the ShapeType enum and the Shape structure, because each different object knows how to draw itself and I don't have to find out what kind of shape it is.

So this draw function uses indirection because I call the draw function on an object. The system will find out what kind of object it is and then call a specific draw function belonging to that object. In this case, each object has a draw function, so I have three different functions with the same name, and the system knows which one belongs to which object.

Notice that there's lots of common code among these classes; in other words, duplicate code. I can combine most of the common code into another class called GeoShape, which will be the parent class of my shape classes.

```
class GeoShape {
    var color : ShapeColor
    var bounds : ShapeRect
    init (bounds : ShapeRect, color : ShapeColor) {
        self.bounds = bounds
        self.color = color
    }
    func draw() {
        println("Drawing basic shape")
    }
}

class Circle : GeoShape {
    override func draw () {
        println("Drawing Circle")
    }
}

class Rectangle : GeoShape {
    override func draw () {
        println("Drawing Rectangle")
    }
}

class Triangle : GeoShape {
    override func draw () {
        println("Drawing Triangle")
    }
}
```

Even though its looks simple, there's a lot going on here.

■   All subclasses inherit the color and bounds instance variables.

■   All subclasses inherit the init and draw functions.

If I didn't implement a specialized function for each of the subclasses, they'd still have a draw function but it would draw only what the basic shape knows how to draw, as shown here.

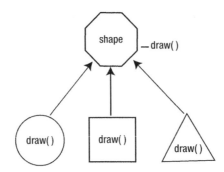

When a subclass implements a function that already exists in the parent class, this is called *overriding* a function. To do this in Swift you have to use the keyword `override` when defining your function. By adding that keyword, you're telling the compiler you know there's an existing function with the same name in the parent class, but you want to provide your own version, so use the function provided by subclass instead of the one from the parent class.

```swift
func drawShapes(shapes : [GeoShape]) {
    for shape in shapes {
        shape.draw()
    }
}
```

I'm passing the base class as the type. This base class defines the basic interface for any class that inherits from it. Each subclass is also a type of its parent class. When I run this program, I still print the correct draw methods, as shown here.

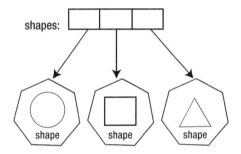

```
Drawing Circle
Drawing Rectangle
Drawing Triangle
```

Now, to add the other type of shape, Hexagon, all I have to do is create a Hexagon subclass of GeoShape and implement the specific draw method to draw a hexagon.

```swift
class Hexagon : GeoShape {
    override func draw() {
        println("Drawing Hexagon")
    }
}
```

And that's it. I don't have to modify anything else. I can just add an instance of Hexagon to the array. I can keep adding more shape types without having to modify the drawShapes function. This is indirection, because what I think is a GeoShape may in fact be a different object. But the compiler knows what type it actually is and makes the correct connection.

Summary

This is a big chapter in the sense that there are lots of new terms and concepts. I talked about indirection, and how you've been using it all along. I showed the limitations of procedural programming, where functions come first and the data follows, and extending that system requires lots of changes and tedious work.

I introduced you to object oriented programming and discussed how it uses indirection, with data first and functions second. I then showed how extending a program by extending existing objects is much easier with OOP.

Chapter 5

Constants, Variables, and Data Types

In OOP languages, an immutable object is an object whose state can't be modified. Swift calls these constants. Once a constant object has been created and an initial value assigned, it can't be changed. In contrast, an object whose value can be changed is a mutable object. Swift calls these variables.

In Swift, variables must be defined and have a valid value before they can be used. Use the var keyword to define a variable and the let keyword to define a constant. Note that all types can be defined either as mutable or immutable (constant or variable) based on whether they're defined with let or var. The language doesn't require separate mutable and immutable types:

```
let numberOfWheelsForBicycle = 2
var numberOfPassengers = 1
```

You can also declare multiple values on a single line:

```
var a = 2.0, b = 5.0, c = 3.0
```

> **Note**   If object values aren't going to change, always declare them as constants using the let keyword.

Type Annotation

So far I haven't provided the type for the variables, since Swift will infer the type from the initial value assigned to the variable. However, you can specify the type of the variable explicitly:

```
var songName : String
```

This line says, declare a mutable variable named songName of type String. I am telling the compiler that songName will store values only of type String. You typically need to do this if Swift can't infer the type of variable.

Once the variable type has been assigned, it can't be changed. You can't declare a variable of type String and then assign a number, even though you haven't assigned an intial value. Once the variable is declared in a scope, you can't redeclare it even with the same type.

Identifiers

The name given to a constant or a variable is called an identifier. Swift was designed to use almost any character, including Unicode characters, for names. However, identifiers can't start with numbers or contain:

- Mathematical symbols (+, -, and so on)
- Arrows
- Private-use Unicode points
- Invalid Unicode points
- Line- or box- drawing characters

```
let Ω = "Omega"
let π = 3.1415
var 🐘 = "Elephant"
var radius = 4.0
var circumference = 2 * π * radius
```

Console Output

Now that you have these values, how do you print them? Swift provides two global functions println and print. The first function prints the variable followed by a line break; the second one prints without appending a line break. The print functions take a string as input. They will print any value that can be converted to a string.

```
println("Hello, This is a long string")
```

To embed a value in a string, you can wrap it with a backslash and parentheses:

```
println("The area of circle = \(areaOfCircle)")
print("Area of Circle = ")
println(areaOfCircle)
```

> **Note**   All string manipulations like this can be used anywhere a string literal is used.

Integers

Almost everyone is familiar with whole numbers. You can define two types of whole numbers, signed or unsigned.

$z = \{\ldots, -3, -2, -1, 0, 1, 2, 3, \ldots\}$

$N0 = \{0, 1, 2, 3, \ldots\}$

Swift provides integers of different sizes based on the number of bits. The ranges of values that can be assigned are based on the size. You can get the min and max value for each of these using the .min and .max functions

```
Int8, Int16, Int32, Int64, UInt8, UInt16, UInt32, UInt64,
println(UInt8.min)
println(UInt8.max)
println(Int8.min)
println(Int8.max)
```

Two other integer types are also available, Int, and UInt. The range of values for these depends on the hardware architecture:

- On 32-bit machines, Int is the same as Int32.
- On 64-bit machines, Int is the same size as Int64.

Similarly UInt is UInt32 on 32-bit machines and UInt64 on 64-bit machines.

Floating-Point Numbers

Floating points numbers are that have fractional parts, such as π, 0.345, and 342.9495. These numbers can represent a much larger set of values. Swift provides two floating point types; the difference is precision.

- Float is defined using 32 bits of data.
- Double is defined using 64 bits of data.

Numeric Literals

You can create numeric literals in various bases using a prefix:

- Decimal numbers have no prefix.
- Binary numbers use the 0b prefix.
- Octal numbers use the 0o prefix.
- Hexadecimal use the 0x prefix.

Floating point literals can be expressed in decimal or hexadecimal. For decimal, the literal comprises a set of decimal digits (with a decimal point). The exponent is a power of 10, separated by the letter "e". 12e2 is the same as $12 * 10^2$ or 1200.0. For hexadecimal, the value starts with the 0x and the exponent is a power of 2, separated by p for power; 0xap3 is same as $0xa * 2^3$ or 40. The exponent can be negative or positive, depending on whether you're multiplying or dividing.

```
var exp0 = 12e2
var exp1 = 0xap2
var exp2 = 12e-2
var exp3 = 0xap-2
```

When writing long numbers, you can separate them using the underscore (_) to make them easier to read. This is purely for human readability. The compiler will strip out the underscore and make a valid number:

```
let million = 1_000_000
let billion = 1_000_000_000
let floating = 1_0.933_39484
```

Conversion

Because one of the central goals of the Swift language is safety, there are only a very few situations where a number's type can be converted automatically. For the most part, you must do an explicit conversion when mixing different types of numbers. The process of converting from one type to another is called casting.

When casting from a larger value to a smaller one, the smaller value won't hold the larger value if it's larger than the maximum value of the smaller. This is called overflow, which in Swift isn't safe, so automatic casting is not allowed most of the time.

If you need to mix numbers of different types, you'll have to convert one of them to the other's type before you can combine them. You can do that by using the constructor for type

```
var ac = million + floating // Error
var ab = million + Int(floating)
```

The expression Int(floating) will convert the floating point number to an integer. This is done by creating an interger from a floating type.

> **Note**   By default, the compiler will create a Double for a floating type. If you actually want a float, you will have to specify the Float type: var myFloat : Float

Booleans

Swift has a Boolean type called Bool, which provides either true or false values.

Characters

Characters in Swift represent a single Unicode character. You can define a character using:

```
let automobile : Character = "🚗"
```

If you don't specify the type, the type inference will create a string type, so for characters you have to either specify the type or express the characters in hexadecimal using the following:

- Single-byte Unicode character \xnn
- Double-byte Unicode character \unnnn
- Four-byte Unicode character \Unnnnnnnn

Strings

Strings are are a sequence of character types.

```
let message = "This is a string"
```

There are special characters that must be specified by escaping with a backslash:

- Null character \0
- Backslash \\
- Horizontal Tab \t
- Line feed \n
- Carriage return \r
- Double Quote \"
- Single Quote \'

To create an empty string, you can define:

```
var string1 = ""
var string2 = String()
```

The String class is fully compatiable with the Objective-C NSString class. You can substitute String for NSString in the API calls, and use methods such as isEmpty, hasPrefix, and hasSuffix on string types.

```
if string1.isEmpty {
    println("This is an empty string")
}
string1 = "Learn Swift on the Mac"
if string1.hasPrefix("Learn") {
    println("The string starts with \"Learn\"")
}

if string1.hasSuffix("Learn") {
    println("The string does not end in \"Learn\"")
}
```

The mutabililty of the strings depends on how they are created. If strings are created using the let keyword they are constants; if they're created using var, strings are mutable.

> **Note** In Objective-C it's different. You use either of two classes NSString and NSMutableString, depending on whether you want a constant or mutable string.

You can concatenate strings and characters with the + operator. You can also use the += to append to an existing string:

```
string1 = string1 + " by Waqar Malik"
string1 += " by Waqar Malik"
```

To count characters, use the global function countElements:

```
let animals = "🐘🐎🐑🐐🐜🐞🐌🐚🐳🐬🐂🐄🐃🐏🐖🐐"
println("Number of characters \(countElements(animals))")
```

To iterate over the characters in the string, you can use the for-in loop (discussed later):

```
for animal in animals {
    print(animal)
}
```

Two strings are considered equal if they have exactly the same characters in the same order:

```
let bookTitle1 = "Learn Swift on the Mac"
var bookTitle2 = "Learn Swift on the Mac"
if bookTitle1 == bookTitle2 {
    println("They are the same")
}

bookTitle2 = "Learn swift on the Mac"
if bookTitle1 == bookTitle2 {
    println("They are the same")
}
```

In the second example, the strings are not the same, because Swift starts with a lowercase character. For computers, S and s are not the same characters.

When comparing strings, if you don't care about the case sensitivity of a string, convert both strings to either uppercase or lowercase and then compare:

```
if bookTitle1.uppercaseString == bookTitle2.uppercaseString {
    println("They are the same")
}
```

Collection Types

Swift provides two collection types, arrays and dictionaries.

Arrays

Arrays store multiple values of the same type in an ordered list. The values can repeated in the list. Arrays in Swift are different from Objective-C:

- Mutability is defined using the let or var declaration.
- All values in the array must of the same type.

> **Note**   NSArray holds objects of type NSObject, which, when imported into Swift, are translated as AnyObject.

There are two ways you can define an array type variable

- `var array : Array<String>`
- `var array : [String]`

The second one is shorthand for creating, in this case, an array of type String. If you try to insert an object of a type other than String, the compiler will give an error.

```
var someFruits : Array<String> = ["Banana", "Apple", "Pear", "Watermelon", "Mango", "Kiwi"]
var someFruits : [String] = ["Banana", "Apple", "Pear", "Watermelon", "Mango", "Kiwi"]
```

You don't have to specify the type if you initialize the array with at least one value so the type can be inferred. The previous declaration can be done by omitting : [String] or : Array<String>:

```
var someFruits = ["Banana", "Apple", "Pear", "Watermelon", "Mango", "Kiwi"]
```

I created an array with the names of some fruits. I can append more items to the array using the append method:

```
someFruits.append("Guava")
someFruits += ["Grapes"]
```

The first line appends one element, and the second line appends an array of one element of the same type.

Use the `isEmpty` property to check if the array is empty:

```
if someFruits.isEmpty {
    println("Array is empty")
} else {
    println("Array is not empty")
}
```

You can retrieve the elements using the subscript syntax:

```
let thirdItem = someFruits[2]
```

As you can see, the arrays use a zero-based index. Since this array is mutable, let's replace some elements. I really wanted grapes instead of bananas:

```
someFruits[0] = "Grapes"
```

You can also replace values in the original array by giving a range. Here are the beginning values: `["Banana", "Apple", "Pear", "Watermelon", "Mango", "Kiwi"]`

To replace items 2 through 4, use:

```
someFruits[2...4] = ["Peaches", "Oranges"]
```

The array now holds these values: `[Banana, Apple, Peaches, Oranges, Kiwi]`

What this did was replace the three items at locations 2, 3, and 4 with two new items, reducing the size of the array by one.

You can increase the size of the array by providing more items on the right side of the expression. The following will increase the size of the original array by replacing the items given by the specified range:

```
someFruits[2...3] = ["Guava", "Plum", "Fig"]
```

After the insertion, the array looks like this:

```
[Banana, Apple, Guava, Plum, Fig, Kiwi]
```

To insert an item at given location in an array use the method `insert`:

```
someFruits.insert("Nectarines", atIndex: 3)
```

To remove an item from the list, use the method `remove`:

```
someFruits.removeAtIndex(1)
someFruits.removeLast()
```

You can iterate over the entire array using a for-in loop:

```
for fruit in someFruits {
    println(fruit)
}
```

If you'd like to get the index of an item along with the item itself, use the enumerate global function on the array. The enumerate function returns a tuple (disussed later) with an index and value for each item:

```
for (index, fruit) in enumerate(someFruits) {
    println("Fruit at index \(index + 1) is \(fruit)")
}
```

You can also create arrays of a given size and a given initial value. To initialize an array of floats of size 10, with initial values of 1.0, you can use a convenience initializer:

```
var myFloats = [Float](count: 10, repeatedValue: 1.0)
// [1.0, 1.0, 1.0, 1.0, 1.0, 1.0, 1.0, 1.0, 1.0, 1.0]
```

Dictionaries

Dictionaries store values of the same type, but they associate each value with a unique key. The keys can't be repeated but the values can be. Think of each key as the index into an array. Unlike with arrays, however, the items don't have an order. For dictionaries you must specify the key type and value type the dictionary will store:

```
var states : Dictionary<String, String> = ["CA" : "California"]
var states : [String : String] = ["CA" : "California"]
```

Both of these define a dictionary states that has a key type of String and value type of String. You don't need to specify the type of the key and value if you initialize the array with values:

```
var states = ["CA" : "California"]
var states = ["CA" : "California", "NV" : "Nevada", "OR": "Oregon", "AZ" : "Arizona"]
```

You can access values of the dictionary by using the key subscript:

```
states["NV"] = "Nevada"
```

or

```
let value = states["NV"]
```

To change the existing value, you set the value using the same key

```
states["NV"] = "State of Nevada"
states.updateValue("State of Nevada", forKey: "NV")
```

Both of these lines update the value of the key "NV", but there's one difference—the updateValue function returns the old value. So you could use:

```
let oldValue = states.updateValue("State of Nevada", forKey: "NV")
```

If the value for the key doesn't exist, these calls will add it to the dictionary. The updateValue function will return nil if key does not exist in the dictionary.

To remove values from the dictionary, you can use the subscript method and assign the nil value to a given key or use removeValueForKey function

```
states["TX"] = nil
```

or

```
states.removeValueForKey("TX")
```

The removeValueForKey function will return the value it replaced or nil if the key doesn't exist.

As with arrays, you can iterate over the entire dictionary using the for-in loop:

```
for (key, value) in states {
    println("State name = \(value), abbreviation = \(key)")
}
```

You can also iterate over just the keys or the values as arrays using the properties keys and values:

```
for abbreviation in states.keys {
    println("Abbreviation = \(abbreviation)")
}

for name in states.values {
    println("Name = \(name)")
}
```

If you'd like to use your own object as a key, the object must hashable; that is, it must conform to the Hashable protocol. This means it must implement a property called hashValue that returns an integer value, a value that identifies the object. A hashValue doesn't need to be unique, but the value does need to be chosen so that objects don't have the same hashValue. The object must also implement the equality (==) operator.

Swift's built-in data types, such as String, Int, Double, and Bool are hashable, which means you can use them for keys.

Tuples

Tuples are groups of ordered values, possibly of different types. You can have named or unnamed tuples, which differ in how you access the elements:

```
let myUnnamedTuple = ("Name", 4.24, 10)
```

This creates a tuple that has three values, and you can see that each is a different type. To acess an individual item in the tuple, you can either reference it by index or by decomposing the tuple to names:

```
println(myUnnamedTuple.0)
println(myUnnamedTuple.1)
println(myUnnamedTuple.2)

let (title, value, other) = myUnnamedTuple
println(title)
println(value)
println(other)
```

You assign a name to each item in the tuple and then access the items using those names. This involves some extra code that's not required if you use named tuple values. To do so, you assign a name to each item in the tuple and then access items using those names:

```
let myNamedTuple = (title: "Name", value: 4.25, other: 10)
println(myNamedTuple.title)
println(myNamedTuple.value)
println(myNamedTuple.other)
```

All of this code is using type inference, but if you want to be explicit about what types the values use you can specify the types:

```
let namedAndTypedTuple : (title : String, value : Float, other : UInt) = ("Name", 4.25, 10)
```

Tuples are useful when you're returning multiple values from functions; you've already seen that with the enumerate function.

Optionals

The concept of optionals is new. There's no equivalent in C or Objective-C—the closest thing is nil in Objective-C. Any type in Swift can be declared optional by adding the ? to the type. But what does that mean?

In Swift, every variable must have a valid value in order to be used, because of the safety requirements of the language. But there are times when you may not have a valid value for a variable. In that case, you declare the variable an optional, meaning that if the variable doesn't have a value, it will be nil; otherwise it will have a valid value. In other words, Int? boxes the value.

```
var myInt : Int? = nil
```

Here myInt is declared as an optional Int and assigned nil as the initial value. If you have valid value, you can simply assign the value to the variable:

```
myInt = 5
```

Now myInt has a valid value of 5, but if you try to use it in an expression, you'll get an error. You have to unbox the optional value before using it. There are two ways to unbox those values:

```
if myInt != nil {
    println(myInt!)
}
```

This uses the ! operator (forced unboxing operator) to access the actual value myInt, telling the runtime I know the variable contains a valid valid and to use it. If you try to use the forced unboxing operator when the variable is nil, that will cause an error at runtime.

The second way is using the if let statement:

```
if let tmpInt = myInt {
    println(tmpInt)
}
```

This is a shortcut for checking whether a variable is not nil and unboxing the value. It assigns a valid value to tmpInt (which is not optional) and now you can use the tmpInt within the if statement.

Summary

These are the basic building blocks (no pun intended) of your programs, along with control structure statements. In every programming language you need these to program efficiently. Pay close attention to the mutability of the objects. Depending on how you declare your variables, they will impact the performance of your program.

I also introduced the powerful concept of optionals, which will help make your programs safe. You don't want to use optionals all the time, but they can be useful when you're not sure a variable will have a valid value.

Chapter 6

Operators

General-purpose languages provide set of operators—convenience constructs that behave like functions—and Swift is no different. You've already seen at least one such operator: +. Swift provides a wide range of built-in operators and allows you to define operators for your own classes and to extend built-in classes to add new operators.

Syntax

Operators in Swift can be:

- Unary, which requires only one operand or input. (-a)

- Binary, which requires two operands or inputs. (a+b)

- Ternary, which requires three operands. (?:)

Notation

Operators come in one of three notations:

- Prefix, where the operator comes before the operand(s). The operator can be either unary or binary. (++a)

- Infix, where the operator requires two operands and comes between them. (a + b)

- Postfix, where the operand(s) come before the operator. The operator can be unary or binary. (a++)

Precedence

Precedence specifies how operators are applied to values in complex expressions. Higher-precedence operators are given higher priority and are evaluated before those with lower precedence. As you know, multiplication has higher precedence than an addition. Suppose you have the expression 1 + 2 * 3. If there were no operator precedence, there'd be two options for evaluating and , depending on which you chose, (1 + 2) * 3 or 1 + (2 * 3), you'd get either 9 or 7. Instead, because multiplication has higher precedence, the answer is always 7 because the multiplication operator is applied to its operands before the addition is. Of course, you can change this binding by using parentheses to set the order. In Swift, precedence is defined by an integer; higher values have higher precedence. Built-in operators have a defined precedence.   Overloaded operator precedence is defined in the declaration.

Associativity

If a statement contains operators with the same precedence, how is that resolved? Look at the expression 1 – 2 + 3. Since both the + and – have the same precedence, you could evaluate this to either 2 or 4, depending which operator you evaluate first. In Swift, mathematical operators have left associativity, meaning that evaluation starts from the left and goes to the right, so that statement is always evaluated as ((1 – 2) + 3).

Swift Operators

Now let's look at the Swift operators, starting with the prefixes, then the infix operators, and finally the postfix operators.

Prefix

- + Unary Plus, +4

- - Unary Minus, -5

- ++ Increment, ++i

- -- Decrement, --i

- ! Logical NOT, !expression (the expression must evaluate to a Bool)

- ~ Bitwise NOT, ~expression (the expression must evaluate to a number)

Infix

Here are the infix operators in order of decreasing precedence.

Bitwise Shift (precedence 160)

Integers are represented as bits. As you know, Int8 is eight bits, so to store 5 you'd have 00000101. If you shift the bits left by 1 bit, you get 00001010, and if you shift the original 00000101 by 1 bit to the right, you have 00000010.

- The left-shift operator is <<. To left-shift a number *n* by *m* bits, you write n << m.

- The right-shift operator is >>. To right- shift a number *n* by *m* bits, you write n >> m.

With unsigned integers, the bit-shifting behavior is as follows:

- Existing bits are moved to the left or right by the requested number of places.

- Any bits that are moved beyond the bounds of the integer's storage are discarded.

- Zeroes are inserted in the spaces left behind after the original bits are moved to the left or right.

The following illustrates shifting an unsigned integer to the left 1 bit:

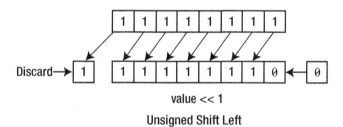

value << 1

Unsigned Shift Left

The following illustrates shifting an unsigned integer to the right 1 bit:

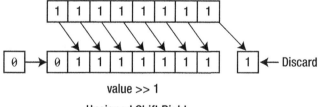

value >> 1

Unsigned Shift Right

```
And this shows the results of some left and right shifts:
let value: UInt8 = 4    // 00000100 in binary
value << 1              // 00001000
value << 2              // 00010000
value << 5              // 10000000
value << 6              // 00000000
value >> 2              // 00000001
```

Signed integers require an extra bit to denote the + or − sign. The first bit reading from left to right (the most significant bit) is used for that purpose; the value 0 indicates a positive number and 1 a negative number. Examples here will use 8-bit numbers, but the principles apply to larger numbers as well.

Negative numbers are stored in two's complement format, which means you subtract the absolute value from 2 to the power of the number of value bits. For 8-bit numbers, the number of value bits is 7, and $2^7 = 128$.

This example represents 4 as a signed integer, first positive and then negative: $128 - 4 = 124$

```
let value : Int8 = 4  // 00000100
let value : Int8 = -4 // 11111100
```

The bit-shifting behavior for signed integers is as follows:

- Shifting left is the same as for unsigned numbers.

- Shifting right is same as for unsigned numbers, but the new signed bit is the same as the previous value to ensure the number keeps its sign.

This illustrates shifting a signed integer with a negative value 1 bit left:

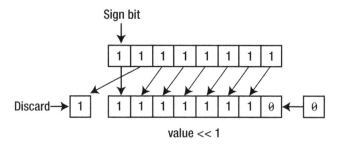

Signed Shift Left Negative Value

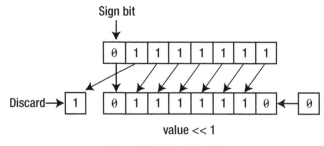

Signed Shift Left Positive Value

This illustrates shifting a signed integer with a negative value right 1 bit:

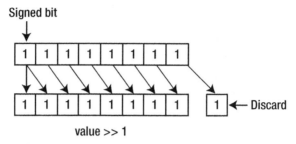

Signed Shift Right Negative Value

This illustrates shifting a signed integer with a positive value right 1 bit:

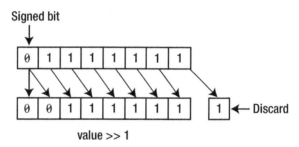

Signed Shift Right Positive Value

Here are some examples:

```
let value: UInt8 = -4  // 11111100 in binary
value << 1             // 11111000
value << 2             // 11110000
value << 5             // 10000000
value << 6             // 00000000
value >> 2             // 11111111
```

Multiplicative (associativity left, precedence 150)

- ▓ * (Multiply)
- ▓ / (Divide)
- ▓ % (Modulus or Remainder)
- ▓ &* (Overflow Multiply)
- ▓ &/ (Overflow Divide)
- ▓ &% (Overflow Modulus or Remainder)
- ▓ & (Bitwise AND)

Additive (associativity, left precedence 140)

- + (Addition)
- - (Subtraction)
- &+ (Overflow Addition)
- &- (Overflow Subtraction)
- | (Bitwise AND)
- ^ (Bitwise XOR)

For safety, there are special operators for handling overflow. By default, Swift will report an error if an operation will result in an overflow. If you use the overflow versions of the operators, you specifically permit the overflow to occur (without error).

Range (precedence 135)

Range operators define a range of values, and Swift has two types of range operators:

- ..< (Half-Open Range)
- ... (Closed Range)

To count all of the numbers in a range, including the first and last, use the closed range operator. If you don't want to include the final value, use the half-open operator. So if you want to include 10 in the range from 1 to 10, you'd use the closed range operator, but if you want to include all the numbers through 9 but not including 10, you'd use the half-open operator.

```
for i in 1..<10 {
    println(i)
}
// prints 1 2 3 4 5 6 7 8 9
for i in 1...10 {
    println(i)
}
// prints 1 2 3 4 5 6 7 8 9 10
```

Cast (precedence 132)

When you convert one object type to another it's called casting. Swift provides two operators: the is operator to check whether the object can be cast to the indicated type, and the as operator to actually cast the value.

```
class Fruit {
}

class Banana : Fruit {
}

var fruit : Fruit = Banana()
if fruit is Banana {
    var banana = fruit as Banana
}
var anotherFruit = Fruit()
if anotherFruit is Banana {
    var banana = anotherFruit as Banana
}
```

The first example shows two types, a parent type called `Fruit` and a subtype called `Banana`. First I create a variable called `fruit` of the explicit type `Fruit`, and then I initialize it with Banana, since banana is also of type `Fruit`. Next I check to see if the type can be cast using the is operator. The statement `fruit is Banana` will evaluate to true and I can have my Banana.

In the second example, `anotherFruit` can't be converted to `Banana` since I initialized it as `Fruit`.

Comparative (precedence 130)

You've already seen most of these operators in other languages and they're fairly self-explanatory. But Swift provides some additional ones.

- < (Less Than)
- <= (Less Than or Equal)
- > (Greater Than)
- >= (Greater Than or Equal)
- == (Equal To)
- != (Not Equal To)
- === (Identical)
- !== (Not Identical)
- ~= (Pattern Match)

When working with reference types, two objects can sometimes point to a single instance of an object. The Swift equal to operator (`==`) checks the values of the objects. To check whether the two variables or constants point to the same instance of an object, you use the identity operator (`===`).

```
if banana === fruit {
    println("they are the same")
}
// prints "they are the same"

if banana !== anotherFruit {
    println("they are not the same")
}
// does "they are not the same"
```

Conjunctive (associativity, left precedence 120)

■ && (Logical AND)

Disjunctive (associativity, left precedence 110)

■ || (Logical OR)

Nil Coalescing (associativity, right precedence 110)

■ ?? (Nil Coalescing)

In Chapter 5 I talked about optional types and how to box and unbox them. The nil coalescing operator can help you write less code when unboxing optional types.

```
var variable1 : String? = nil
var variable2 : String? = "Hello"
var value = variable1 ?? variable2
```

In this example there are two optional variables variable1 and variable2. One has a valid value and the other doesn't. If I were writing this using if statements, I'd check whether variable1 has a valid value and, if so, use that value. Otherwise I'd use the variable2 value. Suppose variable2 does not have a valid value either and I wanted to assign it some default value to the variable value. In a typical if-else statement you would write this as

```
if variable1 != nil {
    value = variable1
} else if variable2 != nil {
    value = variable2
} else {
    value = "Unknown Value"
}
```

In Swift we can use the Nil Coalescing operator and we can write it very concisely

```
var value = variable1 ?? variable2 ?? "Unknown Value"
```

This is a trivial example and you could probably write a simple if/else statement. But what if you had bunch of variables you wanted to get the value from? You could do so simply like this:

```
var value = var1 ?? var2 ?? var3 ?? var4 ?? var5 ?? "Default Value"
```

The code reads as if var1 has a value assigned to it. If it doesn't, the code checks whether var2 has a value assigned to it, and so on until the last, which in this case is "Default Value". The value of the first variable reached that has a valid value will be assigned to value.

Ternary Conditional (associativity, right precedence 100)

- ?: (If-Then-Else Conditional)

Assignment (associativity, right precedence 90)

- = (Assign)
- *= (Multiply and Assign)
- /= (Divide and Assign)
- %= (Modulus and Assign)
- += (Addition and Assign)
- -= (Subtraction and Assign)
- <<= (Left bitshift and Assign)
- >>= (Right bitshift and Assign)
- &= (Bitwise AND and Assign)
- ^= (Bitwise XOR and Assign)
- |= (Bitwise OR and Assign)
- &&= (Logical AND and Assign)
- ||= (Logical OR and Assign)

Postfix

- value++ (Increment)
- value-- (Decrement)

Overloading Operators

Swift lets you use existing operators with your custom types or additional built-in types. To overload an existing operator you define a function that takes the appropriate number of arguments and types for which the operator is overloaded. This is a controversial topic that leads to confusion and ambiguity, and that's bad for programming, which needs to always get the exact same result for the same set of inputs and operations.

Let's say you want to add a string and a number, but what would the end result be? If you wrote the expression "Hello" + 12, what should it produce? Should something like this even be allowed? So think carefully before you start to experiment with operator overloading. Here are some guidelines to help you decide:

- Don't create an operator unless the meaning is clear.

- Operators should be created for convenience. The functionality should be implemented in a separate function the operator function uses.

- Be sure to provide proper precedence and associativity. Try matching the existing operator as closely possible.

- You may also want to create assignment operators if necessary.

Unary Operator

With all that said, let's create an operator, the mathematical symbol Σ which will be used to sum all numbers in an array. It will be a unary prefix operator and will be written as follows:

> **Note**   To type Σ symbol on a OS X system you use the ⌥ (Option, Alt) key and the W key together.

```
var a = [Double] = [30.04, 95.3, 12.9, 0.01, 0.0]
let b = Σa
let b = Σ[30.04, 95.3, 12.9, 0.01, 0.0]
```

Since this is a unary operator, I don't need to worry about precedence and associativity. Creating the new operator is a two-step process: First I declare that it's an operator and then I actually implement the function for it.

```
prefix operator Σ {}
```

- The prefix keyword specifies the type of operator (must be prefix, infix, or postfix).

- The operator reserved keyword indicates it's an operator.

- Σ is the operator itself.

- The braces {} are where you can specify precedence and associativity for infix operators.

Next I define the function that actually does the work. Since this is a `prefix` operator, I start with that keyword, followed by the reserved keyword `func` and then the operator name.

The next steps are to set the kind of arguments the function takes and the kind of value(s) the function returns, and then finally to write the body of the function.

```
prefix func Σ (array : [Double]) -> Double {
    var sum : Double = 0
    for item in array {
        sum += item
    }
    return sum
}
let b = Σ[1.0, 2.0, 3.0] // b = 6.0
let a = [4.0, 5.0, 6.0, 7.0]
let c = Σa // c = 22.0
```

So what happens when the sum overflows? As you know, Swift will mark it as an error, so you should also provide a Σ& operator to handle the overflow conditions.

Binary Operators

There are plenty of binary operators to choose from, ×, ÷, ±, and so on. No doubt you learned as a child that ÷ is divide, so I'm going to make that the new operator.

```
infix operator ÷ { associativity left precedence 150}
func ÷ (left : Double, right : Double) -> Double {
    return left / right
}
```

```
let d = 200.0 ÷ 2 // d = 100.0
```

But if I do that, I get:

```
Var e = 10.0
e ÷= 2
```

I'd get an error, because I haven't created a ÷= operator. Now I'll do that.

```
infix operator ÷= {associativity right precedence 90}
func ÷= (inout left : Double, right : Double) {
    left = left ÷ right
}
```

Left is marked as `inout` because I need to update the value and send it back to the calling function. I'm not done yet—what happens if I divide the left by the value 0? Well, now I have to make the overflow operator ÷&. As you can see, that operator rabbit hole is quite deep, so you need to think carefully about all potential scenarios and make operators that cover most cases.

Summary

These operators come with the Swift standard library. You are probably familiar with most of them from your math classes or from other programming languages. You'll end up using most of them if not all in your programs. When you're creating your own types, you'll probably need some custom operators to help make your types concise and easy to work with.

Sometimes you might want to extend an existing type to provide new operators for convenience, and Swift provides an easy way to do so. When creating your own operators, be careful of the operators that are built into the standard library or the types.

Also keep in mind that when defining custom operators you should follow the well-known conventions and meanings of the operator. Don't define - operator to do addition or + to do division. If you do that, developers will not end up using your types.

Chapter 7

Flow Control

In programming, Control Flow referes to the order of instructions (statements) are executed. Swift provides the standard set of conditional constructs. These include for, while, if and switch, plus break and continue to transfer the control to another location in the code.

Even those these are constrcts are familiar but they provide considerably powerful support for safety.

For Loops

A *for* loop construct provides a way for a block of code to be executed number of times. Swift provides two types of for loops.

- For-in is used in conjunction with objects that are contained in a range, sequence, collection, or progression. These typically include arrays and dictionaries.

- For-conditional-increment performs a block of code until the fail condition is met, usually the fail condition is dependent on a counter.

For-in

You can use the `for-in` loop to iterate over collections (arrays, dictionaries, strings, etc).

Let's start with something simple. We have a range of values that we iterate.

```
for i in 1...6 {
   println(i)
}
```

The above code will print numbers from 1 to 6. The range operator three dots (…) is called a closed range operator, that means that the loop will excute from 1 to 6 inclusive. The value of i is set to first index which in this case is 1, and then the block of code within the curly braces is executed. When the statements in the block are finished, the value of i is updated to the next value in the range, in this case 2, the block is executed again. This process happens repeatedly until end of the range is reached.

Things to notice

- The value i does not need to be declared before it can be used in the for loop.
- i is declared constant for each iteration as if declared with the let keyword.
- The value of i is only available with in the loop block.

We did not specify the type for i by default it will be inferred to be the Int type. If you would like to use another int types such as Int8 or Int16 simply specify like you would when declaring a variable.

```
for i : Int8 in 1...6 {
    println(i)
}
```

> **Note**   Keep in mind that if the range overflows the type then that is an error and Swift will mark it as such.

If you would like to access the value of i outside the loop, then you have to declare it before the loop as a var and then you can modify within the loop and have access outside.

```
Var i = -1
for j in 1...6 {
    i = j
}
println(I)    // prints 6
```

If you do not need the individual values of the range and would like to ignore then you can use the underscore _ instead of the variable.

```
for _ in 1...6 {
    var a = arc4random() % 3
    println(a)
}
```

In languages where arrays are zero based. The index of the first element is 0, so the range is from 0 to n-1 for an array of n elements. To support this, Swift provides a half-closed range operator ..<. In this case the last value in the range is not included.

```
for i in 1..<6 {
    println(i)
}
```

This will only print values from 1 to 5.

As we discussed in the earlier chapter, the curly braces are required for the for loop. This is different from Objecive-C where for a single statement curly braces were optional.

This loop construct comes handy with collections.

```
let animals = ["Dog", "Cat", "Fish", "Lion"]
for animal in animals {
    println(animal)
}
```

For dictionaries, you can use the tuples as the constant values returned from dictionary. Each tuple is a key value pair (key, value), we can decompose the tuple use the explicitly named constants that can be used within the body of the loop.

```
let numberOfWheels = ["car" : 4, "bicycle" : 2, "tricycle" : 3]
for (mode, wheelCount) in numberOfWheels {
    println("The \(mode) has \(wheelCount) wheels")
}
```

In this example we decompose the keys as mode and values as wheelCount constants in the loop.

The items in the dictionaries may not necessoarialy be iterated in the order they were inserted. They contents of the dictionaries depend on the keys, and they are inherently unordered. So the order is not guaranted.

You can also use the for-in loop for strings. Strings are just an ordered collection of characters.

```
for charcter in "Adam" {
    println(charcter)
}
```

For-conditional-Increment

This is the traditional C style for loop.It has general format

```
for initialization; condition; increment {
    statements
}
for var i = 1; i <= 6; i++ {
    println(i)
}
```

The loop execution follows:

1. When the loop is first entered the initialization statement is evaluated.

2. The conditional is evaluated, if the conditional evaluates to false, the loop ends and the block is not executed and the program continutes after the closing curly brace. If the conditional expression evaluated to true, then the block is executed.

3. After the block has executed the increment part is evaluated. After that the execution of the program goes back to step 2 and condition expression is evaluated again.

```
var i = 1
for ; i <= 6; i++ {
    println(i)
}

var i = 1
for ; i <= 6; {
    println(i)
    i++
}
```

Both of the above do the same thing. If you declare the variable as part of the initialization expression such as var i = 0, those variables are only available with the body of the loop, if you need to access those values out side the loop, they must be declared outside the for statement.

```
var i : Int
for i = 1; i <= 6; i++ {
    println(i)
}
println(i)
```

While

The while loop has two parts the condition and the statements. The while loop evaluates the condition and if the condition is true the statements are executed. This is repeated until the condtion evaluates to false, and then the execution of the program continues after the closing curly brace.

```
while condition {
  statements
}
var n = 3456, s = 0, d = 0

while n != 0 {
    d = n % 10
    s = s * 10 + d
    n = n / 10
}
println(s) // 6543
```

Do-while

In do-while loop the condtion is at the end of the loop. That means that statements are always executed at lesast once. The general form is

```
do {
   statements
} while condition

var a = 2, r = 0, n = 45
do {
    r = n % a
    if r == 0 {
        println(a) // 3, 5, 9, 15
    }
    a++
} while a <= n/2
```

Branch Statements

During the execution of your program you need to make choices as to which piece of code need to execute depending on a condition. You call that conditional code. Swift provides you with two ways to handle conditional code, using either the if statement or a switch statement. If is useful when you have limited number of permutation of the conditions. Switch is suited for more complex situations.

If in its simplest form puts a gaurd around statements with a condition and only excute those statements if the condition is true. The parentheses around the condition are not required. The curly braces around the statements are required even if there is only one statement.

```
if condition {
   statements
}
```

> **Note**   In C the condition only needs to be non zero value and it would be considered true. Not in Swift, the condition must evaluate to a Bool type.

```
let a = 10, b = 20
if a < b {
    println("a is smaller than b")
}
```

The code above checks if a is less then b which in this case is true and evaluates to true and the message is printed. If the condition evaluates to false then the message is not printed. The execution continutes after the closing curly brace of the if statement.

If also provides an alternative statement if the condition is not true.

```
if condition {
    statements1
} else {
    statements2
}
```

In this case one of the two sets of statements are executed. If the condtion is true statements1 are executed, if the condtion is false then the statements2 are executed. After execution continutes after last closing brace of the if statement.

```
let a = 20, b = 10

if a < b {
    println("a is smaller than b")
} else {
    println("a is larger than b")
}
```

You can also have multiple brances by chaning additional if statements. You can have zero or more else if conditions. The last else is not required if not needed.

```
if condition1 {
    statements1
} else if condition2 {
    statements2
} else {
    statements3
}
let a = 10, b = 20, c = 30

if a > b && a > c {
    println("a is the greatest")
} else if b > c {
    println("b is the greatest")
} else {
    println("c is the greatest")
}
```

Switch

Sometimes you want to execute one of many different sequences of statements based on the value of a single expression. You can do this by using a set of else if statements, but most languages (including Swift) provide a simpler way to do this.

Swift's mechanism is a `switch` statement. The `switch` statement computes the value of an expression, and then compares it to lists of values to determine what to execute next. The general form is

```
switch condition {
  case value1:
        statements for value1
  case value2:
        statements for value2
  default:
        statements for othervalues
}
```

To match a value it must placed after the `case` keyword. Every switch statement must be exhaustive, that is, every possible value must be considered. Lets say if you are matching against integer values, it is not possible to match every last integer. You can specify a catch-all case called the default. If none of the cases are matched then the statements in the default are executed. The default case must appear at the end of the case list.

```
let character : Character = "r"
switch character {
case "a", "e", "i", "o", "u":
    println("A vowel")
default:
    println("Not a vowel")
}
// Not a vowel
```

There is no explicit fall through for case statements. Every case must provide at least one executable statement. If you do not have any code to execute or just want to exit the switch statementusethe break statement to leave the switch. The following code will give you can error, becase the first four cases do not have any statements (and there is no fall through).

```
let character : Character = "r"
switch character {
case "a":
case "e":
case "i":
case "o":
case "u":
    println("A vowel")
default:
    println("Not a vowel")
}
```

If you would like to fall through explicity, you have to use the keyword fallthrough. The above code can be correctly written as:

```
let character : Character = "a"
switch character {
case "a":
    fallthrough
case "e":
    fallthrough
case "i":
    fallthrough
case "o":
    fallthrough
case "u":
    println("A vowel")
default:
    println("Not a vowel")
}
```

You can also match multiple values in a case by separating them with a comma.

```
Let character : Character = "a"
switch character {
case "a", "e", "I", "o", "u":
    println("a vowel")
default:
    println("not a vowel")
}
```

Range Matching

You can also use the range operators in the case statemnts.

```
let number = 300000
switch number {
case 0 ..< 10:
    println("Units")
case 10 ... 99:
    println("tens")
case 100 ... 999:
    println("Hundreds")
case 1000 ... 999_999:
    println("thousands")
case 1_000_000 ..< 1_000_000_000:
    println("millions")
case 1_000_000_000 ..< 1_000_000_000_000:
    println("billions")
default:
    println("a vary large number")
}
```

Tuples

You use tuples to test the multiple values in the same switch statement; each element in the tuple can be tested for a different value or range of values. If you would like to match any value in a tuple you can use the _ as the matching parameter.

```
let latlon = (36, -77)
switch latlon {
case (0, -180...180):
    println("On the equator!")
default:
    println("Not on the equator")
}
```

The above case statement will match to make sure that first item in the tuple matches to 0 and the rest of it maches between -180 to 180 for the second value. If the first value does not match then the second value is will be ignored.

Value Binding

The switch statement can bind values to temporary constants that can be used withing the body of the switch. A case with value binding matches all possible values for that value.

```
let latlon = (36, -77)
switch latlon {
case (0, let lon):
    println("On the equator at longitude \(lon)!")
case (let lat, let lon):
    println("At latitude \(lat\) and longitude \(lon\)")
}
```

String Matching

Not only can match individual charcters but can you match strings in the case statement.

```
let carMaker = "Porsche"

switch carMaker {
case "BMW", "Porsche", "Audi", "VW":
    println("German")
case "Toyota", "Nissan", "Mazda":
    println("Japanese")
case "GM", "Ford":
    println("American")
default:
    println("Unknown")
}
```

Where Clause

You can use the where clause in the case expression to check for additional conditions.

```
let fraction = (10, 20)
switch fraction {
case let (num, 0):
    println("dividing by zero")
case let(num, den) where num % dem == 0:
    println("the fraction represents a whole numbe \(num/dem)r")
case let (num, den):
    println("non whole number \(num) over \(den)")
}
```

We first decopose the fraction to its individual items in the tuple for each case, the first case we check if the denominator is a 0 we and error, the next we check if the remainder (% operator) is zero that means the numerator is a multiple of the denominator. The last case matches every thing.

Control Transfer Statements

When you need to change the order of execution of your program you can use one of the four statements.

Continue

The continue statement in the body of the loop tells the loop to skip the rest of the statements in the loop and go to the biginining of the loop.

```
var odds = [Int]()
for i in 1...20 {
    switch i {
    case let a where a % 2 == 0:
        continue
    default:
        odds.append(i)
    }
}

println(odds)
```

We just want filter out odd numbers from 1 to 20, we use our switch statement to test if the number is even if it is even then we continue to the next iteration of the loop. Any statements after continue are skipped over and the execution goes to the top of the loop.

Break

Break stops the execution of the entire control flow statement. Break can be used in loops and switch statement.

When break is used within a loop, the execution of the loop stops immediately at the break statement and falls out of the loop and the execution of the program continus after the close curly brace (}) of the loop.

```
for i in odds {
    if i == 11 {
        break
    }
    println(i)
}
```

In this simple example we iterate over our odd numbers, and we the number until we get to 11 and then we are done. As soon as we match 11 we stop the execution of the for statement.

Break in switch ends the execution of the switch statement and continue of the program with at the closing brace (}). Some times it is useful that you don't want to execute a statement after matching a case in the switch statement you can use break to end it

```
enum Suit {
    case Diamonds
    case Hearts
    case Spades
    case Clubs
}
let hand = Suit.Diamonds

switch hand {
case .Diamonds:
    println("Diamonds")
case .Hearts:
    println("Hearts")
case .Spades:
    println("Spades")
case .Clubs:
    println("Clubs")
default:
    break
}
```

Because that every case must have one executable statement, since we did not want to print any message we just used break statement.

Fallthrough

The switch statement do not fall through to the next case statement, instead once the statements in a particular case are executed the switch statement ends and the flow continues out side of the switch statement. You have to explicitly note that after executing the current case statements continue to match the next case statements.

```
switch hand {
case .Diamonds:
    println("Yippie")
    fallthrough
case .Hearts:
    println("Got Red card")
case .Spades:
    fallthrough
case .Clubs:
    println("Got Black card")
default:
    println("Got Joker")
}
```

In this example we print both "Yippie" and "Got Red Card"

Return

The return statement is used in functions to end the execution of the function and skip the rest of the statements in the function. A typical scenario is checkin if the arguments of the function are valid before continue with the fuction.

```
func myfunction(input1 : Int?) {
    if nil == input1 {
        return
    }

    println("We executing function")
}
```

Labeled Statements

You can have nested switch stetements and loops, some time it is import to explicitly halt or skip a specific loop or switch block. Swift allows you to label loops and switch statement so you can explicitly break or continue a particular loop or switch

```
label-name : while  condition  {
    statements
}
```

Use this label after either break or continue. We can rewrite our earlier for loops

```
oddsloop : for i in 1...20 {
    switch i {
    case let a where a % 2 == 0:
        continue oddsloop
    default:
        odds.append(i)
    }
}

oddsloop1 : for i in odds {
    if i == 11 {
        break oddsloop1
    }
    println(i)
}
```

Keep in mind that label is only available in the scope of the loop or switch statement.

Summary

Control flow is what helps use write complex programs. Swift provide a rich set of stements that allows you to do:

- Execute set of statement only certain condition is met.
- Execute set of statement zero or more times.
- Skipping set of statements.

We saw lots of examples how switch can help us achive our goals. Specifically the switch statement in Swift it has become very powerful. It can match strings, range of values, have clauses in cases, or wild card matches.

Chapter 8

Functions and Closures

Functions are self-contained blocks of code that perform a specific task. Swift's functions are very flexible. They can be very simple, such as the `println` or `print` functions, or very complex.

- They can be simple C-style functions with no parameter names.

- They can have local and external parameter names for paramters, similar to Objective-C.

- They can have parameters that provide default values.

- They can return multiple values.

- They can be passed as arguments.

- They can be returned as a result from other functions.

- They can have nested functions.

Defining Functions

The general format for a function starts with the keyword `func`, followed by the name of the function, optional arguments, and an optional return value.

```
func functionName([Parameters]) [-> returnValue] {
}
```

Items within the brackets [] are optional. Let's define a simple function called `greeting`:

```
func greeting(name : String) -> String {
    let greetingMessage = "Hello " + name
    return greetingMessage
}
```

This function takes one argument of type `String` and has a return value of type `String`. The body of the function prepends the word Hello to a name.

Calling a Function

To execute the code that the function represents is called "calling" a function. To call a function, you simply use the name of the function and any arguments that are required.

```
greeting("Waqar")
```

This calls the example function with an argument. Since I didn't capture the return value from the function, it's simply discarded. You can assign the result of the execution to a variable:

```
let mygreeting = greeting("Waqar")
```

You can also specify multiple arguments by separating each argument with a comma:

```
func greeting2(name1: String, name2 : String) -> String {
    let greetingMessage = "Hello " + name1 + " and " + name2
    return greetingMessage
}
let greeting2Message = greeting2("Waqar", "Adam")
```

You can also have a function without any parameters:

```
func greeting0() -> String
{
    return "Hello, Swift"
}
let greeting0Message = greeting0()
```

Sometimes you want functions that don't return values. You don't need to specify the return type. In that case, the default is a return value Void.

```
func greeting3(name: String) {
    println("Hello " + name)
}
greeting("Waqar")
```

The return value is of type Void. If you wanted to be pedantic, you could write a function that actually returns a value of Void. The following code is equivalent to the preceding code:

```
func greeting3(name: String) -> Void {
    println("Hello " + name)
}
```

> **Note**   Void is just an empty tuple, with no elements, that's written as ().

A function that's defined to have a return value must always return a value of given type. If you'd like to return a nil, the return type must be defined as an optional.

Functions can return multiple values. To do this, you must use the tuple type to box multiple values and return them:

```
func greeting4(name1 : String, name2 : String) -> (String, String) {
    let greeting1 = "Hello " + name1
    let greeting2 = "Hello " + name2

    return (greeting1, greeting2)
}
var greetings : (greeting1 : String, greeting2 : String) = greeting4("Waqar", "Mishal")

println(greetings.greeting1)
println(greetings.greeting2)
```

Parameter Names

All the functions I've defined have parameters names, such as name1 and name2. These names are available only within the body of the function; they can't be accessed outside of the function. These are called local parameter names.

The functions that defined my caller function are unaware of the parameters. However, it can be useful for the caller function to know the purpose of the arguments. To solve this issue, Swift allows external parameters names that you can give to each parameter along with the local parameters.

You specify the external parameter name before the local parameter name. Once you've defined the external parameter name, that name must be used when calling the function.

```
func greeting5(firstPersonName name1: String, secondPersonName name2 : String) -> String {
    let greetingMessage = "Hello " + name1 + " and " + name2

    return greetingMessage
}

let greeeting5Message = greeting5(firstPersonName: "Waqar", secondPersonName: "Mishal")
```

In this case, the local name and the external name are different. It's generally a better idea to use the external name as the internal name because that describes the parameter better. Doing that, the function looks like this:

```
func greeting2(firstPersonName: String, secondPersonName : String) -> String {
    let greetingMessage = "Hello " + firstPersonName + " and " + secondPersonName

    return greetingMessage
}
```

But this doesn't provide an external name. Let's add that:

```
func greeting2(firstPersonName firstPersonName: String, secondPersonName secondPersonName :
String) -> String {
    let greetingMessage = "Hello " + firstPersonName + " and " + secondPersonName

    return greetingMessage
}
```

But that's kind of tedious. Wouldn't it be nice to have to type the parameter names just once? Yes! To do this, you can just start the parameter name with #.

```
func greeting2(#firstPersonName: String, #secondPersonName : String) -> String {
    let greetingMessage = "Hello " + firstPersonName + " and " + secondPersonName

    return greetingMessage
}

let greeting2Message = greeting2(firstPersonName: "Waqar", secondPersonName: "Adam")
```

Default Values

You can define default values for parameters when defining your function. If the default value for a parameter is defined, the parameter name can't be omitted when calling the function, but you can omit the parameter completely when calling if you would like to use the default value.

```
func greeting(name : String = "Waqar") -> String {
    let greetingMessage = "Hello " + name
    return greetingMessage
}

let mygreeting = greeting()
let mygreeting = greeting(name: "Mishal")
```

The first call will use the default value for the name and the second one will pass the value as an argument.

> **Note**   Arrange the parameter list in such a way that the parameters with default values are at the end, so that the order of parameters looks the same for nondefault values when omitting default parameters.

You can opt out of this behavior by defining the external name with an underscore (_). In that case, you don't have to call the function with an external name, but this is not a recommended practice.

Variadic Parameters

Some times you need a function that can take an unknown number of arguments. You can use three periods ... to specify a variadic parameter, which can take zero or more values. The arguments are made available inside the function as an array of the specific type.

```
func sum(numbers : Double...) -> Double {
    var sum = 0.0
    for number in numbers {
        sum += number
    }

    return sum
}

let mysum = sum(3.0, 5.0, 6.0)
```

> **Note** Functions can have only one variadic parameter, and it must always come at the very end of the parameter list. If the function has parameters with default values, the variadic parameter must come after all the defaulted variables, at the very end of the list.

Mutablity of Parameters

By default, parameters are passed as constants and you can't change their values within the body of the function. Sometimes it is nice to be able to reuse a variable instead of defining a new one. To do so, you simply prefix the parameter with the var keyword:

```
func greeting(var name : String = "Waqar") -> String {
    name = "Hello " + name
    return name
}
```

> **Note** The changes made to the variable within the body of the function are available only within the function. They don't persist outside the fuction.

In-Out Parameters

If you'd like a parameter's value to exist outside the function, it must be marked as such using the inout keyword. When passing the variable to an inout parameter, the variable must be prefixed with ampersand (&).

```
func tripleit(inout value : Double) {
    value *= 3
}
```

```
var value = 2.0
tripleit(&value)
println(value) // 6.0
```

Some restrictions apply to inout parameters. These parameters can't

- have default values,
- be variadic,
- be passed a constant,
- be passed a literal, or
- be marked as var or let.

Function Types

When you define a function, its type is also created; the function types are made up of the arguments and return types.

```
func add(x: Double, y : Double) -> Double {
    return x + y
}
func multiply(x : Double, y : Double) -> Double {
    return x * y
}
```

These two functions have the same type; they have two arguments of type Double and return an argument of type Double. You write the function type as (Double, Double) -> Double. If you have a function that has no arguments and doesn't return a value, the type for that function is () -> ().

```
func myFunc () {
// Some computation
}
```

Now that you know that functions have a type, you can define a variable that can hold functions. I can use the type of the two math functions I defined earlier and define a variable. Then I can use that variable as a function.

```
var mathFunction : (Double, Double) -> Double
mathFunction = add
var result = mathFunction(3, 4) // 7

mathFunction = multiply
result = mathFunction(3, 4) // 12
```

Functions as Parameters

Since the variable is defined to take a specific type, you can make a new function that has the same type and assign it to this variable. You can also pass the function as an an argument to another function.

You define the function parameters as you'd define any other parameter:

```
func compute(#computeFunction: (Double, Double) -> Double, #x : Double, #y : Double) ->
Double {
    return computeFunction(x, y)
}

result = compute(computeFunction: multiply, x: 3, y: 4)
```

In this function, I define the first argument as the function needed to compute the result;the other two are the values the function will take.

Functions as Return Values

You can take this one step further and have functions return other functions. Just define the return value for the function as a function type:

```
func computeFunction(#type : String) -> ((Double, Double) -> Double) {
    if(type == "+")
    {
        return add
    } else if type == "*" {
        return multiply
    } else {
        func myRand(x: Double, y : Double ) -> Double {
            return 42.0
        }
        return myRand
    }
}

mathFunction = computeFunction(type: "+")
result = mathFunction(3, 5)
```

Nested Functions

Most of the functions I've defined are global in scope, meaning they are available to everything in the module to use. In the previous example I defined a function named myRand within a function. That function is only available to be called within the function computeFunction. By combining all the preceding functions into one function, I have:

```
func computeFunction2(#type : String) -> ((Double, Double) -> Double) {
    func localAdd(x: Double, y : Double) -> Double {
        return x + y
    }

    func localMultiply(x : Double, y : Double) -> Double {
        return x * y
    }

    func myRand(x: Double, y : Double ) -> Double {
        return 42.0
    }

    if(type == "+")
    {
        return localAdd
    } else if type == "*" {
        return localMultiply
    } else {
        return myRand
    }
}
```

Closures

Closures are blocks of code that perform specific tasks; they can be passed around in your code. Closures in Swift are similar to blocks in C and Objective-C and to lambdas in some languages. Closures can capture and store references to constants and variables in the context in which they are defined. This is called "closing over" these constants and variables. Swift handles all the memory management required for capturing the environment.

The definition for closures is similar to that for functions, because in Swift functions are a special case of closures, with some differences:

- Global functions are closures that have a name and don't capture any values.

- Nested functions are closures that have a name but only capture values from the enclosing function.

Swift closure syntax is very clean with

- Inferred types for parameters and return types
- Implicit return from a single statement
- Short-hand argument names
- Trailing closure syntax

Closure Syntax

```
{ ( parameters ) -> returnType in
        statements
}
```

Parameters can be of type:

- Constant
- Variable
- Inout
- Variadic (only if it's the last parameter)
- Tuple

Let's take look at the global function called `sorted` in the standard Swift library. The function takes two arguments:

- An array with known types for elements.
- A closure that takes two arguments of same type as the array elements and returns a Boolean. If the the result is true, the first value will stored before the second value in the new array. If the result is false, the second value will be stored before the first value.

The simplest and best-known way to handle this is to create a function that has the same signature as the closure and pass that as an argument. If you've used any of the sorting functions built into the C library, such as qsort, you know those functions have as their last argument a comparator function.

```
let numbers : [Int] = [119, 11, 45, 9, 34, 202]
func asending(element1 : Int, element2 : Int) -> Bool {
    return element1 < element2
}

let sortedNumbers = sorted(numbers, asending)
```

The problem with this is you have to define each function ahead of time. Let's try this with a closure.

```
let sortedNumbers = sorted(numbers, {(element1: Int, element2 : Int) -> Bool in
    return element1 < element2
})
```

The inline closure looks almost identical to the function. I just removed the name, moved the arguments within the curly braces, and added the `in` keyword to denote the start of the closure block.

Inferring Types from Context

Since I defined the closure inline with the `sorted` function, the compiler can infer the types of the argument and the closure, so I don't have to specify them. Because I don't need to specify the types, I can also omit the parentheses and `->` from the arguments and just specify the names of the arguments. My code is now even simpler:

```
sortedNumbers = sorted(numbers, { element1, element2  in
    return element1 < element2
})
```

Implicit Returns

If the closure has one statement in the body and that one statement computes the return value of the closure, the closure can implicitly return that value and you can omit the return keyword.

```
sortedNumbers = sorted(numbers, {element1, element2 in element1 < element2})
```

Shorthand Argument Names

The arguments in an inline closure are automatically given internal names $0, $1, and so on, depending on the number of arguments. You can use those instead of the names you define. If you decide to use these names, you can omit the argument list and the `in` keyword as the inference system will correctly determine them. Then, the closure is made up solely of its body.

```
sortedNumbers = sorted(numbers, { $0 < $1 })
```

Trailing Closures

If the function takes a closure as the final argument, you can move the closure expression outside of and after the parentheses. That's why it's recommended that you use trailing closures when defining functions.

```
sortedNumbers = sorted(numbers) { $0 < $1 }
```

Capturing Values

I mentioned earlier that closures will capture variables and constants within the scope in which they are defined. The simplest example of this are nested functions:

```
func capturingValues() {
    var a : Double = 5
    println(a)
    func increment(incrementBy : Double) {
        a += incrementBy
    }

    increment(4)
    println(a)

    increment(2)
    println(a)
}
```

Notice that I don't pass variable a into the body of the function, but the function still has access to the variable. I defined the function after defining the variable. In this case, the variable was captured because it was in the scope of the function when it was defined. If I define any variables after the function is defined, they won't be captured because they are not in the function's scope when the function was defined.

```
func capturingValues() {
    func increment(incrementBy : Double) {
        a += incrementBy
    }
    var a : Double = 5
    println(a)

    increment(4)
    println(a)

    increment(2)
    println(a)
}
```

This code would cause the Swift compiler to give an error because the variable was not in scope when the function was defined.

Summary

A function is a set of instructions that performs a specific task. It's a way to generalize functionality because it can be called mutltiple times or from different locations. In object-oriented programming, functions that belong to a specific object are called methods, but in Swift, methods are also declared using the `func` keyword.

You might already be familiar with the concept of closures. In Objective-C, they are called blocks. In Swift, blocks are imported as closures so you can use the two interchangeably. In Swift, functions are just named closures. You have to pay close attention to how closures capture the state of a program and how they can lead to memory cycles. You should be mindful when you use instance variables within closures.

Chapter 9

Classes and Structures

In Chapter 4 you learned about object-oriented programming (OOP), and how an object can be represented in Swift as a class, a structure, or an enumeration type.

Unlike in other languages, in Swift classes and structures are very similar, with only few features that separate them. So as I describe and discuss the functionality of objects, this applies to both classes and structures. I'll point out where they differ.

Commonality

Here are some of the things classes and structures have in common:

- Properties to store values
- Methods to provide functionality
- Initializers
- Extensibility
- Conformance to protocols

Classes have some additional properties and capabilities that structures lack:

- Inheritance; classes can have parent classes, structures can't.
- Deinitialzers; classes have them, structures don't.
- Reference counting; classes use reference counting to manage memory.
- Runtime support for type casting.
- Classes are passed by reference while structures are copied when passed around.

Some languages use two files for classes, one for the interface and one for the implementation. Like Java, Swift uses only one file, which a .swift extension. You generally create one file per class or structure and give it the same name as the class. If I'm creating a Person class, I'd name the file Person.swift.

> **Note**   Unlike Objective-C, Swift classes don't require a parent class. And use single inheritance for class hierarchy.

Definition

You use either the class or struct keywords, depending on whether you're creating a class or structure. Here's the syntax:

```
class [name of class] {
        // class definition
}

struct [name of struct] {
        // struct definition
}
```

When you define a struct or class in Swift, you're creating a new data type. Swift follows the UpperCamelCase format for names for types; they start with an uppercase letter and each successive word also starts with uppercase letter, for example, MyType, SomeFancyType. This is a convention but not a requirement. Now let's look at a struct:

```
struct Point {
    var x = 0.0
    var y = 0.0
}
```

I define a structure called Point that has two properties called x and y. I defined x and y as variables, but you can also have constants using the let keyword. I initialized the values to some good default values. The types are inferred to be double by the compiler. Let's keep going:

```
class Engine {
    var numberOfCylinders : Int = 4
}
```

Here's a class named Engine. For now, its only property is the number of cylinders; I gave it a default value of 4.

I've only defined the two new types; they have to be instantiated before I can use them. The syntax for creating an instance of either a class or a struct is same:

```
var location = Point()
var smallEngine = Engine()
```

Accessing Properties

Both of the objects I defined have some properties. To access them you can use the dot (.) syntax.

```
println(smallEngine.numberOfCylinders)
println(location.x)
```

> **Note** Access control restricts access to certain parts of the code, which allows you to hide implementation details of your types. I'll discuss access control at length in another chapter. For now, I'll use the default access control for types.

Here's how you assign new values to properties:

```
smallEngine.numberOfCylinders = 5
location.x = 10
location.y = 30
```

You can drill down into the properties and access them

```
class Automobile {
    var engine = Engine();
    var numberOfWheels = 4
}
var car = Automobile()
car.engine.numberOfCylinders = 6
```

Value Types vs. Reference Types

A value type is a one whose value is copied when it's assigned to a variable or when passed as a function parameter.

```
var anotherLocation = location
location.x = 20
location.y = 50

println(location.x) // 20
println(anotherLocation.x) // 10
```

When I assign the point value to anotherLocation, Swift creates a copy of the object and assigns the existing values from the location object. If I change the value of the original location, I won't affect the value of the new variable.

> **Note**   All basic types in Swift are value types. They are implemented as structures.

Reference types are types whose values are not copied. Instead a reference to an existing object is copied. Classes in Swift are reference types.

```
let myCar = car
car.engine.numberOfCylinders = 10
println(myCar.engine.numberOfCylinders)
```

This code creates another variable called myCar, which refers to the existing object. When I change the value of numberOfCylinders for the original car, I also change the values of the properties of myCar. Those properties point to the same location in memory that holds the original car.

But, you say, myCar is declared as a constant. How can you change the value of a constant? With reference types you define the variable that it points to to be a constant. In this example, myCar can't point to any other car. If you try something like myCar = Car(), you'll get an error, because you're trying to point to another location.

> **Note**   Reference types in Swift are similar to pointers in C/C++/Objective-C. They are better in Swift in that you don't have to use the dereference operator (*).

Now you know that classes in Swift are reference types, and that it's possible to have multiple variables point to same object. How can you find out if two variables point to the same instance of the object? Swift provides two operators:

- Identical to (===)
- Not identical to (!==)

```
if myCar === car {
    println("Both myCar and car are the same instance of the Car")
}
```

The identity operator (===) is different from the equality operator (==). Suppose you and your friend go to the Apple store and purchase identical iPhones. The phones are equal (==) to each other because they have the same feature set, but they are not the same phone so the identity operator would fail.

Choosing Between Classes or Structures

Most of the time you'll want to create classes for your objects, but there are few situations where you should use structures instead.

- If you want to copy the object when passing it around.
- If the properties of the object themselves are value types.
- If the object doesn't inherit from other types.

If you were building a tree data structure, you'd want the node to be a structure, and the tree itself to be a class.

What if you don't want your nested class to be used only within the enclosing class? Swift provides three levels of access control.

Properties

I already used properties in an example, but only one type of property so far. There are actually two types of properties:

- *Stored properties* store some values for an instance of your class.
- *Computed properties* compute the values.

> **Note**   Enumerations can't use stored properties, only classes and structures can.

Stored Properties

In the Engine class example, I've one stored property called numberOfCylinders. Stored properties can be either mutable using the var keyword or immutable using the let keyword. I also provided a default value for the property. You can override these default values during the initialization of the class, even for let keyword properties.

```
class Engine {
    let numberOfCylinders : Int = 4

    init(numberOfCylinders: Int) {
        self.numberOfCylinders = numberOfCylinders
    }
}
```

The property numberOfCylinders is set in the init method (more on init later); if you try to set the value outside the init method, Swift will give an error.

Lazy Stored Properties

Sometimes you need to wait to calculate the value of a stored property until the initialization has taken place. You mark such properties with the lazy keyword. These properties are useful when the functionality may never be used.

> **Note**   Lazy properties must be of var type, as they might be initialized outside of the init methods.

```
class Automobile {
    lazy var engine = Engine(numberOfCylinders: 6)
    var numberOfWheels = 4
}
```

In the preceding code, I marked the engine property as lazy, even though I initialize it with the init method. The init method won't be executed until I access the engine property. Now look at the following:

```
class Engine {
    let numberOfCylinders : Int = 4
    init (numberOfCylinders : Int) {
        self.numberOfCylinders = numberOfCylinders
        println("Engine Init function Called \(self.numberOfCylinders)")
    }
}

class Automobile {
    var engine = Engine(numberOfCylinders: 4)
    var numberOfWheels : Int = 4
}

class Automobile2 {
    lazy var engine = Engine(numberOfCylinders : 6)
    var numberOfWheels : Int = 4
}

func create () {
    var car1 = Automobile()
    var car2 = Automobile2()
}

create() // Engine Init function Called 4
```

Because I don't access the car2 engine, it's never created.

Computed Properties

These properties don't store any values. Instead, they provide a getter and a setter to provide values based on other properties. The syntax for these properties is:

```
var propertyName : PropertyType {
  get {
     return someValue
  }
  set(value) {
  }
}

class Automobile {
    class Engine {
        let numberOfCylinders : Int = 0
        var started : Bool = false
        init(numberOfCylinders: Int) {
            self.numberOfCylinders = numberOfCylinders
        }
    }
    let engine : Engine
    let numberOfWheels : Int

    var started : Bool {
        get {
            return self.engine.started
        }
        set(started) {
            self.engine.started = started
        }
    }
    init (numberOfCylinders : Int, numberOfWheels : Int) {
        engine = Engine(numberOfCylinders: numberOfCylinders)
        self.numberOfWheels = numberOfWheels;
    }
}

var fastCar = Automobile(numberOfCylinders: 6, numberOfWheels: 4)
println("Car started \(fastCar.started)") // false
fastCar.started = true
println("Car started \(fastCar.started)") // true
```

You can skip the argument declaration for the setter. Swift will automatically create a variable called newValue and you can access that within the setter.

```
set {
    self.engine.started = newValue
}
```

If you provide a getter but no setter, the computed property becomes a read-only property. Even though it's a read-only property, it's not a constant and can't be declared as such with the let keyword.

Property Observers

You can add property value change observers to any stored property. These observers are called whenever a new value is set, even if the value will remain the same. Observers are not called when a property is first initialized.

> **Note**   You can't add property observers to lazy stored properties.

You can also add observers to inherited properties; they can be either stored or computed by overriding them in a subclass.

You can implement either or both of the following observers on a property:

- willSet is called before the value is changed.
- didSet is called after the value is changed.

The following code shows both:

```
class Engine {
    var numberOfCylinders : Int = 0 {
        willSet(cylinderCount) {
            println("about to set the cylinder count \(cylinderCount)")
        }
        didSet {
            println("engine now has \(self.numberOfCylinders) cylinders")
        }
    }
    var started : Bool = false
    init(numberOfCylinders: Int) {
        self.numberOfCylinders = numberOfCylinders
    }
}
```

You can omit the new value argument in the willSet observer if you want. In that case, you can access the new value by using the variable name newValue.

The didSet observer doesn't provide an argument for the old value, but you can still access it using the oldValue variable within the observer:

```
class Engine {
    var numberOfCylinders : Int = 0 {
        willSet{
            println("about to set the cylinder count \(newValue)")
        }
        didSet {
            println("engine had \(oldValue) cylinders")
    println("engine now has \(self.numberOfCylinders) cylinders")
        }
    }
    var started : Bool = false
init(numberOfCylinders: Int) {
        self.numberOfCylinders = numberOfCylinders
    }
}
```

Type Properties

All the properties I've used are instance properties because they belong to a specific instance of the object. If you create an engineA and an engineB, both will have their own properties called numberOfCylinders that aren't shared between the two. The syntax is:

```
struct MyStruct {
        static var storedTypeProperty = "Some Value"
        static val computedProperty : Int {
                return someInt
        }
}

enum MyEnum {
        static var storedTypeProperty = "Some Value"
        static var computedProperty : Int {
                return someInt
        }
}

class MyClass {
        class var computedProperty : Int {
                return someInt
        }
}
```

To access those properties, you use the dot syntax, and you use the object type instead of an instance of the type, like so:

```
println(MyStruct.storedTypeProperty)
MyStruct.storedTypeProperty = "New Value"
```

Summary

In object-oriented programming in Swift, custom objects or types are the basis of programs. In Swift, even basic types such as Int and Double are value types and are defined as structures, which allows you to extend basic types with your own convenience functions.

You learned the difference between value types and reference types, and saw how to choose the best solution for your specific problem. You also learned what properties are and how to use them effectively.

Chapter 10

Methods

A subroutine is a block of code that performs a specific task. Another name for a subroutine is a function. You've already seen global functions, such as `println` and `print`. Methods are functions that are associated with a particular type. In Swift, methods can be associated with classes, structures, and enumeration types. There are two types of methods: instance methods and type methods.

Instance Methods

Instance methods are those that belong to a particular instance of a class. You have to create an object to use those methods. They are defined just like standalone functions, but within the class scope:

```
class Stack {
    private var stack = [Double]()

    func empty () -> Bool {
        return self.stack.count == 0
    }

    func peek () -> Double? {
        return self.stack.last
    }
        func pop () -> Double? {
        let value = self.stack.last
        if nil != value {
            self.stack.removeLast()
        }
        return value
    }
```

```
    func push (item : Double) {
        self.stack.append(item)
    }
}
```

The Stack class implements four instance methods and a property that stores the values for the stack.

To use the instance methods, you create an instance of the Stack and then use the dot notation to invoke methods:

```
var stack = Stack()
// crate a new instance of stack

println(stack.empty())
// check if the stack is empty prints true

stack.push(5)
// push a value of 5 on top of the stack

println(stack.empty())
// Check if the stack is empty prints false

var value = stack.peek()
// See what value is the top of the stack

stack.push(103)
// push another value

value = stack.pop()
// get the top value
```

The argument names for methods have the same rules as for functions, except that, by default, Swift gives the first parameter name in the method a local parameter name, and the second and subsequent parameter names the local and external names. Basically, you don't need to add the extra name or # as part of the parameter name.

To call an instance method within another method, you can use the dot notation and the self keyword. The use of self is optional—it's inferred. The only exception is when the parameter name is the same as the method name, in which case the parameter name takes precedence.

> **Note**   Self is a special property that gets created for each instance of the type. It refers to that specific instance of the type and can only be used within that instance.

I can rewrite the class like this:

```
class Stack {
    private var stack = [Double]()

    func empty () -> Bool {
        println("local Empty")
        return stack.count == 0
    }

    func peek () -> Double? {
        return stack.last
    }

    func pop () -> Double? {
        let value = stack.last
        if nil != value {
            stack.removeLast()
        }
        return value
    }

    func push (item : Double) {
        stack.append(item)
    }
}
```

Modifying Type State

One of the differences between classes, as opposed to structures and enumeration types, is that in structs and enums methods by default don't allow modifying of the state or the values of properties.

```
struct SomeStruct {
    var value = 0.0
    func updateValueBy(someValue : Double ) {
        value = value + someValue
    }
}
```

In this example, the updateValueBy function is trying to update the property value but this is not allowed. You can opt-in to the mutating behavior of the method by prefixing the method with the mutating keyword.

```
struct SomeStruct {
    var value = 0.0
    mutating func updateValueBy(someValue : Double ) {
        value = value + someValue
    }
}
```

You can't call mutating methods for structures declared as constants. The following code would result in an error; because myStruct is defined using the let keyword, it's immutable.

```
let myStruct = SomeStruct()
myStruct.updateValueBy(10)
```

In structures, you can even assign a new value to self in mutating methods.

```
struct SomeStruct {
    var value = 0.0
    mutating func updateValueBy(someValue : Double ) {
        self = SomeStruct(value + someValue)
    }
}
```

The mutating methods of an enumeration type can set the self to a different member value of the type.

```
enum SomeEnum {
    case value1, value2
    mutating func toggle () {
        switch self {
        case value1:
            self = value2
        case value2:
            self = value1
        }
    }
}
var myEnum = SomeEnum.value1
myEnum.toggle()
```

Type Methods

Type methods are those that belong to a particular type. You don't need to create a specific instance of an object to use those. For classes, you use the keyword class before a method definition and for a struct you use the static keyword. And to call those methods, you use the type name instead of a particular instance of type.

```
class SomeClass {
    class func typeMethod() {

    }
}
```

```
SomeClass.typeMethod()

struct SomeStruct {
    static func staticFunc () {
    }
}

SomeStruct.staticFunc()
```

Summary

Methods are the basis for creating and extending types. They help you structure code in a reusable set of instructions. There are two types of methods: instance methods and type methods. Methods are the interface to the types; they help you hide the implementation details. You can override methods in subclasses or extend the existing type by adding methods. This allows you to make a type very versatile, so you can avoid writing duplicate code.

Access Control

Access control is a feature of programming languages that restricts access to code based on where it's defined. You can apply access control to the following items:

- Classes
- Structures
- Enumerations
- Properties
- Initializers
- Methods

Some limited support for access control is available for:

- Protocols
- Global functions
- Global constants and variables

Most of the time, you won't have to specify the access level. Swift provides a default access level that works in most cases.

Modules and Source Files

First, I'm going to introduce a few terms, because to some extent the access control you get depends on how the code is structured. Access control applies at the module and source file level.

A source file in Swift is a single file in which you create your code. Typically, you create a source file for each type (class, struct, and so forth), but you can create multiple types, functions, and more.

A module in Swift is a set of files compiled into a single executable, which may be either a framework or an application. For example, if you create an iOS/OS X application that consists of multiple files and compile those files into one executable, that's a module. You can also take code that's common among multiple applications and create a framework that can be imported into your application using the `import` keyword.

Access Levels

Swift provides three levels of access control, from least restrictive to most restrictive:

■ *Public* access allows access between modules. If, for example, you are creating a framework and you use public types and methods, anybody who imports your module can use these.

■ *Internal* access allows access within a given module. This is the default level if you don't specify the access level explicitly.

■ *Private* access allows access only within the file type. This is typically used to hide the implementation details of entities (that is, properties, types, functions, and so forth).

From one entity, you can only define entities with a more restrictive access level.

■ You can't define a public class that has a parent class that's internal or private. But you can define a class that's private from a public or internal class.

■ You can't define a public property on a class that's declared as internal or private.

■ Functions can't have a more restrictive access level than their arguments or return values.

Note   Some languages, like C++ and Java, have an access level called protected. Swift doesn't provide protected access. C++ also has private and public access levels.

Syntax

Swift has three keywords that can be used to define the access level: `private`, `internal`, and `public`.

```
public class MyPublicClass {}
internal class MyInternalClass {}
private class MyPrivateClass {}

public var myPublicVariable = 0
internal let myInternalConstant = 1
private func MyPrivteFunction() {}
```

If you leave out the `internal` keyword, the compiler will give default access level of `internal`.

Classes

You have to give the access level of a class as part of its definition, and this access control affects the class's properties, methods, subscripts, and initializers.

```
private class MyPrivateClass // explicitly private
{
    var myProperty = 0 // implicitly private

    func MyFunction() { // implicitly private


    }
}

class MyInternalClass // explicitly internal
{
    var myInternalProperty = 0  // implicitly internal
    internal var myOtherInternalProperty = 5 // explicitly internal
    private var myPrivateProperty = 4 // explicitly private

    func MyInternalMethod() { // implicitly internal
    }

    private func MyPrivateFunction () { // explicitly private
    }
}

public class MyPublicClass { // explicitly public
    var myPublicProperty = 9 // implicitly internal
    public var myProperty = 7 // explicitly public
    internal var myInternalProperty = 8 // explicitly internal
    private var myPrivateProperty = 5 // explicitly private

    func myFunc1() { // implicitly public
    }

    public func myFunc2 () { // explicitly public
    }

    internal func myFunc3 () { // explicitly internal
    }

    private func myFunc4() { // explicitly private
    }
}
```

Subclassing

You can only subclass parent classes that are visible within your current context. All subclasses of a parent class must have an access control level equal to or stricter than that of the parent. You can't subclass a public or internal class from a private parent class. Furthermore, you can only override class members (methods, properties, subscripts, and initializers) that are visible in a certain context.

```
public class MyOtherClass : MyPublicClass {
    public override func myFunc3 () {
    }

    internal override func myFunc4() {
    }
}
```

Class Members

Constants, properties, subscripts, and variables can't have a higher access level than that of the type they're declared in. You can't define a public property for a private class. A subscript can't be more public than its index type or the return type. If one of these entities makes use of a private type, that entity must also be marked as private.

```
private var myPrivateVar = MyPrivateClass()
```

Functions

The access level for the function is calculated from the function's parameters and return types, using the most restrictive level.

```
func MyFunction () -> (SomePublicType, SomePrivateType) {
// return a tuple
}
```

Since I didn't specify an explicit access level for this function, you'd assume the default level of `internal` would be assigned. But that's not case, because the return value of the function is a `tuple` composed of two distinct types. One type is defined with public access and the other with private, so the overall access level of the tuple is private. Since the return type of the function is private, the function must be declared as private.

```
private func MyFunction () -> (SomePublicType, SomePrivateType) {
// return a tuple
}
```

Enumerations

The case types for enumerations get the same access level as the enumeration and can't be changed.

```
public enum MyEnum {
    case Left
    case Right
}
```

The access level for .Left and .Right are implicitly public and can't be changed to private or internal.

The types used by the raw values in an enumeration must have an access level as high as the enumeration's. If the enumeration has an access level of internal, you can't use a private access level for raw types, but you can use an internal or public access level.

Nested Types

Nested types defined within a private type are automatically private, but types defined within public or internal types are always internal. If you need to have private access to a type defined in a public type, you have to explicitly mark the item.

```
public class MyPublicClass { // explicitly public
    class MyInnerClass { // implicitly internal
    }
}

public class MyPublicClass { // explicitly public
    public class MyInnerClass { // explicitly public
    }
}
public class MyPublicClass {
    private class MyInnerClass {
        func myInnterFunction() {
            println("Inner Function")
        }
    }
    func myFunction() {
        println("myFunction")
        myInnerClass.myInnterFunction()
    }

    private var myInnerClass = MyInnerClass()
}
```

Getters and Setters

Getters and setters by default get the same access level as the member they belong to. If you have a public property, for example, the getter and setter will also have public access levels.

You can give a setter stricter access than the getter, if you want to make a read-only property, for example.

```
public private(set) var myPublicProperty = 9
```

This gives the setter private access and the getter as public access.

> **Note**   This rule applies to both computed and stored properties.

Initializers

Custom initializers can be defined with an access level less than or equal to the type they are initializing. The only exception is the required initializer must have the same access level as the class it belongs to. Also, the parameters for the initializer can't be more private than the initializer itself.

Swift provides a default initializer (an initializer without any arguments) if you don't define at least one initializer for the type. The default initializer will have the same access level as the type it initializes, unless the type is public. If the type is defined as public, the default initializer is defined as internal. If you want to give explicit public access, you must define a no-arguments initializer with a public access level as part of the type definition.

Protocols

You can assign an access level at the time you define a protocol, so the protocol can only be accessed for a given context. The access level of each item within the protocol is set to the same level as the protocol itself, and the access level can't be changed for these items. When the protocol is implemented, the items receive the access level that was defined for the protocol.

If a protocol inherits from another protocol, the new protocol can have at most the same level as its parent. If a protocol inherits from an internal protocol, for example, you can't implement a public subprotocol; it must be private or internal.

A type can conform to a protocol that has a lower access level than the type itself, so an internal class can implement a public protocol. If you have a public type that implements an internal protocol, only internal types can be used in the module where the protocol is defined.

Extensions

When you extend a class, structure, or enumeration, the access level of the extension defaults to the same level as that of the original type. If you're extending a public type, then all types in the extension will have internal access. You can extend types using an explicit access level. For example, if you want to extend a public class to have just a private extension, you can do so using the private access level `private extension`. You can also set the access level for each member of the type.

> **Note**   You can't provide an explicit access level if you're implementing a protocol in an extension. In that case, the access level of the protocol is used.

Typealias

Type aliases will have an access level less than or equal to the type it is being used to alias. You can make a private or internal alias of a public type, but you can't make a public alias for an internal or private type.

Summary

You learned how to properly allow access to the types you define or when you extend existing types. When in doubt, think of a security-clearance model where a lower level of clearance can't access a higher level of security. In Swift, private is the highest level of protection and public means no protection at all.

Chapter 12

Inheritance

When you write an object-oriented program, the classes and objects you create have relationships with one another. They work together to make your program do its thing.

Two aspects of OOP are most important when dealing with relationships between classes and objects. The first is **inheritance**, the subject of this chapter. When you create a new class, it's often useful to define the new class in terms of its differences from an already existing class. Using inheritance, you can define a class that has all the capabilities of a parent class: it *inherits* those capabilities. You can have a general class called Automobile, for example, that defines a vehicle for operation on roads, typically with four wheels, such as a truck or car. Automobile can define some basic properties that constitute an automobile, and then you can create a specialized automobile by defining a Car type that will inherit from Automobile. It will get its properties from Automobile so you don't have to redefine them. You only add new properties that make it a car. This is inheritance because Car inherits the Automobile's properties.

The other OOP technique used with related classes is **composition**, in which objects contain references to other objects. For example, a car object in a racing simulator might have four tire objects it uses during game play. When your object keeps references to others, you can take advantage of features offered by the others; that's composition.

Terminology

- **Superclass** or **parent class** is the class you are inheriting from.
- **Subclass** or **child class** is the class that is inheriting.
- **Override** is when you replace the implementation of a method in the parent class with a method in the child class.
- Any class that does not inherit from a class is called a **base class**.

> **Note**   Unlike Objective-C, Swift classes do not require a common parent base class such as
> NSObject.

Defining a Base Class

Let's define a base class called Shape that we'll use to extend and draw specific types
of shapes:

```
class Shape {
    var fillColor : UIColor
    var bounds : CGRect

    init(bounds : CGRect, fillColor : UIColor) {
        self.bounds = bounds
        self.fillColor = fillColor
    }

    func draw () {
        println("I don't know how to draw this shape.")
    }
}
var shape = Shape(bounds: CGRectZero, fillColor: UIColor.redColor())
shape.draw()
```

This class has two properties, the fill color and the bounding box, and a method called
draw to draw the desired shape. In the base class I don't draw any shape because I have to
create a specialized class that knows how to draw the shape.

Subclassing

Swift only allows single inheritance, which means that a subclass can only have a single
parent class. Some languages, notably C++, allow multiple inheritance in which a child class
can have more than one parent class.

The syntax for Swift subclassing is simple: when defining a subclass you add a colon and
then the name of the parent class.

```
class Subclass : Superclass {
}
```

Let's extend the Shape class and specialize it to draw a circle

```
class Circle: Shape {
}

shape = Circle(bounds: CGRectMake(0.0, 0.0, 30.0, 30.0), fillColor: UIColor.blueColor())
shape.draw()
```

I defined a new class called `Circle` that has the `Shape` parent class. `Circle` inherits the bounds and `fillColor` properties of the parent class. It also inherits the `draw` method and my initializer method as well. I'll use the `init` method from the parent class because I don't need to change it. But I'm going to override the `draw` method to draw my circle.

Any method that's internal or public can be overridden; you just need to add `override` before the definition of the method.

```
class Circle: Shape {
    override func draw() {
        println("Drawing a circle in a bounding box \(NSStringFromCGRect(self.bounds)) and
color \(self.fillColor.description)")
    }
}
```

The following items can be overridden in Swift

- Instance methods

- Type methods

- Instance properties

- Type properties

- Subscripts

Let's create another subclass of the Shape class and call it `Polygon`.

```
class Polygon : Shape {
    var numberOfSides : Int = 3
    override func draw() {
        println("Drawing a polygon with \(numberOfSides) sides in a bounding box
\(NSStringFromCGRect(self.bounds)) and color \(self.fillColor.description)")
    }
}

shape = Polygon(bounds: CGRectMake(0.0, 0.0, 30.0, 30.0), fillColor: UIColor.blueColor())
shape.draw()
```

If you want to access the superclass's methods from the subclass, you replace the reference to `self` with `super`. Let's say a user sets the number of sides to an invalid value and the program doesn't know how to draw the polygon. You could ask the parent to draw the shape, but in this case the parent doesn't know how to draw so it simply prints that message. You can also use super with any other method.

```
class Polygon : Shape {
    var numberOfSides : Int = 3
    override func draw() {
        if numberOfSides <= 0 {
            super.draw()
        } else {
```

```
        println("Drawing a polygon with \(numberOfSides) sides in a bounding box \
(NSStringFromCGRect(self.bounds)) and color \(self.fillColor.description)")
        }
    }
}
```

Properties

You can override the getters and setters for inherited properties or add custom observers. The overriding of the getters and setters works with both stored and computed properties. The subclass doesn't know if the inherited property is stored or computed. To override, you have to specify both the name and the type of the property.

For inherited properties that are read-only in the superclass, you can provide both setter and getter to make the property read-write. If a property is read-write in the super class, you can't make is read-only in the subclass.

You can't add property observers to inherited constant stored properties or inherited read-only computed properties. You can't provide both an overriding setter and an overriding property observer for the same property. Simply observe it in the setter. The following example shows how to override properties to observe and to provide a custom setter and getter.

```
class Circle: Shape {
    override var fillColor : UIColor {
        didSet {
            println("the new color is \(self.fillColor)")
        }
    }

    override var bounds : CGRect {
        get {
            return super.bounds
        }
        set (newBounds) {
            super.bounds = CGRectInset(newBounds, 5, 5)
        }
    }

    override func draw() {
        println("Drawing a circle in a bounding box \(NSStringFromCGRect(self.bounds)) and
color \(self.fillColor.description)")
    }
}
```

Preventing Overriding

All this freedom is good, but sometimes you want to prevent those using your code from overriding some parts. You can do that by marking your methods, properties, classes, and subscripts as final:

- `final func`
- `final class func`
- `final var`
- `final subscript`

You can even mark a whole class as final to prevent users from subclassing.

```
final class Myclass {
}
```

Any attempt to override or subclass items marked with the final keyword will result in an error.

Summary

You learned a key concept in object-oriented programming called inheritance. Inheritance provides a powerful way to design and modularize programs. When you start to develop your programs, you will be extending classes and methods to customize them for your needs.

Chapter 13

Extensions

When you write object-oriented programs, you'll often want to add some new behavior to an existing class. For example, you might have designed a new kind of tire, so you'd subclass Tire and add the new, cool stuff. When you want to add behavior to an existing class, you often create a subclass.

But sometimes subclassing isn't convenient. For example, to add some new behavior to String, you can sublass the string as your own string type such as MyString, but what if you're using a toolkit or library they will have no knowledge of this new new class. When the toolkit or library return a string it will be returned as the original string type, you will end up converting those String type to MyString every time if you wanted to use new functionality in your string class.

The dynamic runtime dispatch mechanism employed by Swift lets you add methods to existing classes. The Swift term for these new methods is **extensions**.

You can add extensions to classes, structures and enums. Since basic types such as Int are structs, you can even extend them and add functionality.

> **Note** Extensions are analogous to categories in Objective-C. However, in Objective-C, each category must have a name, while in Swift extensions don't have names.

With extensions you can:

- add computed properties
- add static computed properties
- add instance and type methods
- add initializers

- define subscripts
- define and use new nested types
- make an existing type conform to a protocol

Note   Extensions can't override existing functionality; they can only add new functionality.

Creating an Extension

The syntax for adding an extension to an existing type is:

```
extension ExistingType {
    // your additions
}
```

To extend an existing type to conform to one or more protocols, simply specify the protocols as you'd define a class or structure:

```
extension ExistingType : Protocol1, Protocol2 {
    // protocol additions
}
```

If you look that the Apple definition for Array structure, they have added an extension to the base Array structure, and one of the function they have added is removeLast

```
/// Remove an element from the end of the Array in O(1).
/// Requires: count > 0
mutating func removeLast() -> T
```

Apple has not defined a function that removes the first element,. Let's add that convenience method:

```
extension Array {
    mutating func removeFirst() -> T {
        let firstObject = self.removeAtIndex(0)
        return firstObject
    }
}
```

Since I added this method, it will be available to all instances of Array types even if they were created before I added this method.

Computed Properties

Extensions can add computed instance and type properties to existing types. Look at the class Circle from Chapter 12. If I want to extend Circle to return the area of the circle or the circumference, I can add couple of computed properties. Since I defined this class, I could just add these as a normal method. If I didn't have access to the implementation or wanted to separate the implementation, I could use an extension.

```
let π = 3.141
extension Circle {
    var radius : Double {
        let width = Double(self.bounds.size.width)
        return width / 2.0
    }

    var area : Double {
        let radius = self.radius
        return (p * radius * radius)
    }
}
```

I defined two properties—the first one computes the radius of the circle and the second one then computes the area of the circle.

Since these are read-only properties, I don't define the set methods. Extensions can't add stored properties or add observers to existing properties.

Initializers

Extensions can add new initializers to existing types. This gives you the power to initialize types with your custom types that the system doesn't know about.

> **Note**   Extensions can't add designated initializers or deinitializers to the class.

Let' say you defined a type that you need to initialize as an existing type. You could just initialize the existing type and then assign different values, but you'd have to do that every time you create a new type. Or you could just define an initializer that encapsulates that logic.

```
extension UIColor {
    convenience init(rgba : UInt32) {
        let r = CGFloat(Double(rgba >> 24 & 0xFF) / 255.0)
        let g = CGFloat(Double(rgba >> 16 & 0xFF) / 255.0)
        let b = CGFloat(Double(rgba >> 8 & 0xFF) / 255.0)
        let a = CGFloat(Double(rgba & 0xFF) / 255.0)
```

```
        self.init(red: r, green: g, blue: b, alpha: a)
    }
}

let color = UIColor(rgba: 0xff0000ff)
```

In this example I define an extension to `UIColor` to take an unsigned integer and create a color instance.

> **Note**   When you define an initializer in an extension, you are still responsible for making sure that each instance is fully initialized once the initializer completes.

Methods

You've already seen how to add methods. You can add both instance methods and type methods to an existing type.

Using my convenience `init` method I can extend the `UIColor` class some more by adding a type method.

```
extension UIColor {
        class func colorWithRGBAHex(rgba : UInt32) -> UIColor? {
                return UIColor(rgba: rgba)
        }
}
let color = UIColor.colorWithRGBAHex(0x00ff00ff)!
```

Mutating Methods

If the type you're adding with the extension is a structure or an enumeration type and you need to modify the state of the object, you must use the mutating keyword just as you would when adding methods when creating the original type.

You saw earlier that I added a method to an `Array` type. Because the `Array` type is defined as a struct in Swift and not as a class, I had to add the `mutating` keyword in front of the method.

In Swift, the basic `Int` type is a structure. I can even extend it by adding some methods:

```
extension Int {
    mutating func doubleIt() {
        self = 2 * self
    }
}

var myint = Int(5)
myint.doubleIt()
```

Subscripts

Extensions can add a subscript to existing types. You saw an example of a Stack type in chapter 10. Suppose you wanted to peek at the nth element from the top if it exists. You could do so with the following:

```
extension Stack {
    subscript(index : Int) -> Double? {
        if self.stack.count < index {
            return self.stack[index]
        }
        return nil
    }
}
var stack = Stack()
stack.push(5)
stack.push(103)
println(stack[1])
```

Nested Types

With extensions you can even add nested types to existing types (classes, structures, and enumerations). This example adds the error type enum to UIColor to return a color based on the error type. I added a new type called ErrorType.

```
extension UIColor {
    enum ErrorType : Int {
        case Normal, File, API
    }

    class func errorColor(errorType : ErrorType) -> UIColor? {
        var color : UIColor? = nil
        switch errorType {
        case .Normal:
            color = colorWithRGBAHex(0xff0000ff)
        case .File :
            color = colorWithRGBAHex(0xcc0000ff)
        case .API:
            color = colorWithRGBAHex(0xaa0000ff)
        }

        return color
    }
}

var color = UIColor.errorColor(.API)!
color = UIColor.errorColor(.Normal)!
```

Summary

Now you know how to extend existing types with extensions. You can tell from these simple examples that extensions are very powerful compared to categories in Objective-C. If you look at the source of the Swift standard library, you'll notice that it makes extensive use of extensions. For instance, the Array type has at least eight different extensions. Typically, each extension conforms to a protocol, which makes it easy to factor your code. Also, extensions don't have names as they do in Objective-C, which makes it easier to work with them.

Chapter 14

Memory Management and ARC

Memory management is part of a more general problem in programming called resource management. Every computer system has finite resources for a program to use. These include memory, open files, and network connections. If you use a resource, such as by opening a file, you need to clean up after yourself (in this case, by closing the file). If you keep on opening files but never close them, you'll eventually run out of file capacity. Think about your public library. If everyone borrowed books but never returned them, eventually the library would close because it would have no more books.

Of course, when your program ends, the operating system reclaims the resources it used. But as long as your program is running, it uses resources, and if you don't practice cleanliness, some resource will eventually be used up and your program will probably crash. Moreover, as operating systems evolve, the notion of when a program actually ends is becoming fuzzy.

Not every program uses files or network connections, but every program uses memory. Memory-related errors are the bane of every programmer who uses manual memory management. Our friends in the Java and scripting worlds have it easy: memory management happens automatically for them, like having their parents clean up their rooms. We, on the other hand, have to make sure to allocate memory when we need it and free that memory when we're finished with it. If we allocate without freeing, we'll leak memory: our program's memory consumption will grow and grow until we run out of memory and then the program will crash. We need to be equally careful not to use any memory after we free it. We might be using stale data, which can cause all sorts of errors, or something else might have moved into that memory, and then we end up corrupting the new stuff.

> **Note**   Memory management is a difficult problem. Swift's solutions are rather elegant but do take some time to wrap your mind around. Even programmers with decades of experience have problems when first encountering this material, so don't worry if it leaves your head spinning for a while.

Object Life Cycle

Objects within a program have a life cycle. They're born (via new); they live (receive messages and do stuff), make friends (via composition and arguments to methods), and eventually die (get freed) when their lives are over. When that happens, their raw materials (memory) are recycled and used for the next generation. When an object is created, you do so using one of the defined initializers, and when the object is destroyed the deinitializer is called. You can do any work that's required during the creation and destruction of the object.

Reference Counting

Now, it's pretty obvious when an object is born, and I've talked a lot about how to use an object, but how do you know when an object's useful life is over? Swift uses a technique known as reference counting, also sometimes called retain counting. Every object has an integer associated with it, known as its reference count or retain count. When some chunk of code is interested in an object, the code increases the object's retain count, saying, "I am interested in this object." When that code is done with the object, it decreases the retain count, indicating that it has lost interest in that object. When the retain count goes to 0, nobody cares about the object anymore so it's destroyed and its memory is returned to the system for reuse.

> **Note**   Reference counting only applies to instances of classes, and not to structures or enumeration types. Structures and enumeration types are value types, not reference types. Value types are copied every time they're assigned or passed, so each value object is a distinct item.

Object Ownership

Reference counting doesn't seem hard. What's the big deal? You create an object, use it, release it, and memory management is happy. That doesn't sound terribly complicated, but things get more complex when you factor in the concept of object ownership. When something is said to "own an object," that something is responsible for making sure the object gets cleaned up.

An object with instance variables that point to other objects is said to own those other objects. That's called a strong reference. It means you have a firm hold on that object, and it will not be released until you let go of that hold.

ARC

Automatic Reference Counting, or ARC, is a compile-time system that keeps track of and manages the memory an application uses. ARC is pretty smart; most of the time you don't have to worry about allocation and deallocation of memory.

To illustrate how ARC works, let's start by creating a simple class called Student, into which I'll put some debug statements so I can see what's going on.

```
class Student {
    let name : String
    init(name : String) {
        self.name = name;
        println("Student \(self.name) is being initialized")
    }

    deinit {
        println("Student \(self.name) is being deinitialized")
    }
}
```

> **Note** If you wish to experiment with this, you can use a playground, which I discuss in Chapter 2. Playground objects remain allocated after their retain count indicates they are no longer used so they can be examined for debugging. If you want to try these examples, create a command-line tool project and step through it with the debugger.

As you can see, in the init method I print the student's name and a message saying that student is being initialized. And I also added a deinit method so I could print a message when the object goes away.

The following code creates an instance of Student and assigns it to the variable student. Now the variable student has a strong reference.

```
var student : Student? = Student(name: "Adam Malik")
// prints Student Adam Malik is being initialized
```

If I assign a nil to student, I give up the strong reference and the system will reclaim the memory.

```
student = nil
// prints Student Adam Malik is being deinitialized
```

Now let's create some more references to the variable by creating more objects and assigning the existing object to them

```
var student : Student? = Student(name: "Adam Malik")
var student1 : Student? = student
var student2 : Student? = student
```

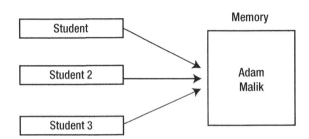

Now there are three strong references to the original object. When I run this program, I don't get a deinit message. Even if I assign nils to student and student1, the object is still not released because student2 still has a strong reference. However, if I assign nil to all three objects, there are no strong references to the student object and the system will release it.

Strong Reference Cycles

The previous example is simple and straightforward and ARC can correctly manage the memory. But most programs you'll write aren't that simple. In the next example I'll create two new classes called Driver and Automobile.

```
class Automobile
{
    let name : String
    init(name: String) {
        self.name = name
    }

    var driver : Driver? = nil;
    deinit {
        println("Automobile \(name) is being deinitialized")
    }
}

class Driver
{
    let name : String
    init(name : String) {
        self.name = name
    }

    var automobile : Automobile? = nil
    deinit {
        println("Driver \(name) is being deinitialized")
    }
}
```

Notice that the Driver type has an optional property called automobile and the Automobile type has an optional property called driver. Let's create a car and a driver. Both of these variables have a strong reference and so far they are independent of each other; if I were to nil them out, they'd just go away.

```
var mario : Driver? = Driver(name: "Mario Andretti")
var ferrari : Automobile? = Automobile(name: "Ferrari")
```

Now let's assign a driver to the automobile instance and an automobile to the driver
instance:

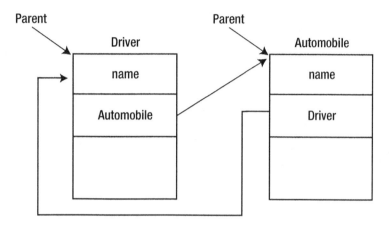

```
mario!.automobile = ferrari
ferrari!.driver = mario
```

By doing this, the Driver instance has a strong reference to the Automobile instance and
the Automobile instance has a strong reference to the Driver instance. If I were to nil out the
mario object and the ferrari object, unfortunately I wouldn't get deinit messages. Both
of these instances have two strong references and by niling the original variables, I only
decreased the references by 1. They still have one more reference, and since it is not zero
that memory is still in use. This is called a cycle. Because I lost the original references, I no
longer have access to that memory and now I also have a memory leak.

Resolving Strong Reference Cycles

How can I solve this problem? Swift provides two ways to resolve cycles: weak references
and unowned references.

Both of these references enable instances of types to refer to other instances without having
a strong hold on them. In this case, the driver and automobile types can refer to each other
without having a cycle. What's the difference between these two types of references and
when do you use them?

- Use a weak reference whenever it's valid for that reference to become nil
  at some point during its lifetime.

- Use an unowned reference when you know that the reference will never
  be nil once it has been set during initialization.

Weak References

A **weak reference** is reference that does not have a strong hold on the instance it refers to. This behavior is very useful in preventing reference cycles. To indicate a weak reference, use the keyword weak before a property or variable declaration.

There are some requirements for using a weak reference:

- It must be declared as a variable using the var keyword.

- It can't be declared as a constant.

- It must be declared as optional.

When the instance the weak reference refers to goes away, ARC will set the value of the reference to nil. This allows you to check whether the reference is nil before using it.

In my example, it's possible for the driver to not have an automobile, so I can declare the automobile property to be weak.

```
class Driver2
{
    let name : String
    init(name : String) {
        self.name = name
    }

    weak var automobile : Automobile2? = nil
    deinit {
        println("Driver \(name) is being deinitialized")
    }
}

class Automobile2
{
    let name : String
    init(name: String) {
        self.name = name
    }

    var driver : Driver2? = nil
    deinit {
        println("Automobile \(name) is being deinitialized")
    }
}
```

Now I create two instances of the types and assign some values. I have an instance of Driver2 that has a strong reference. Also, renault has a strong reference to the Automobile2 instance. After I assign some values to the references, I have another strong reference to the Driver instance but a weak reference to the Automobile instance. When I'm done with driver and automobile, I can get rid of them and ARC will correctly clean up the memory.

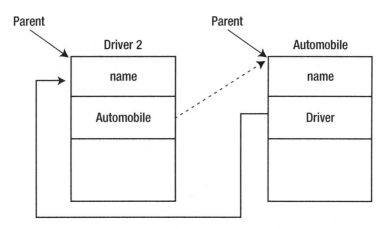

```
var vettel : Driver2? = Driver2(name: "Sebastian Vettel")
var renault : Automobile2? = Automobile2(name: "Renault")
vettel?.automobile = renault
renault?.driver = vettel

renault = nil
vettel = nil
// Automobile Renault is being deinitialized
// Driver Sebastian Vettel is being deinitialized
```

Unowned Reference

Just like weak references, unowned references don't have a strong reference to the instance they refer to. The difference is that an unowned reference must always have a value. You define the unowned reference by using the unowned keyword. With regard to unowned references

■   They can't be declared as optional.

■   ARC can't set the value to nil.

If you access the value of an unowned reference after its instance has been deallocated, you'll get a runtime error and your program will crash.

I'm going to extend the example. Let's say a Person may or may not own an automobile but an automobile must have an owner, so I make the automobile property of the Person object optional and a weak reference, but the owner property of the automobile unowned. Since Automobile must have an owner, I have to create an automobile by passing the name and the owner values to the initializer.

```
class Person
{
    let name : String
    init(name : String) {
        self.name = name
    }

    var automobile : Automobile3? = nil
    deinit {
        println("Person \(name) is being deinitialized")
    }
}

class Automobile3
{
    let name : String
    init(name: String, owner: Person) {
        self.name = name
        self.owner = owner
    }

    weak var driver : Person? = nil
    unowned var owner : Person
    deinit {
        println("Automobile \(name) is being deinitialized")
    }
}

var waqar : Person? = Person(name : "Waqar Malik")
var vw : Automobile3? = Automobile3(name: "Volkswagen", owner: waqar!)
waqar?.automobile = vw
```

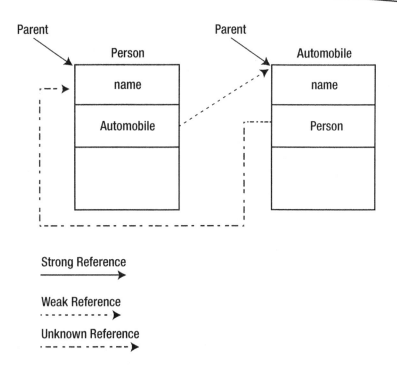

I have a strong reference to automobile for Person, and a weak reference to owner.

Strong Reference Cycles and Closures

You've already seen that having strong references can lead to strong reference cycles where you leak memory. You also know that closures capture the environment around them, which can cause strong reference cycles quite easily.

A strong reference cycle can occur if you assign a closure to a property of a class instance, and the body of that closure captures the instance. This capture might occur because the closure's body accesses a property of the instance, such as self.someProperty, or because the closure calls a method on the instance, such as self.someMethod. In either case, these accesses cause the closure to "capture" self, creating a strong reference cycle.

This strong reference cycle occurs because closures, like classes, are reference types. When you assign a closure to a property, you are assigning a reference to that closure. In essence, it's the same problem as the one described earlier—two strong references are keeping each other alive. However, rather than two class instances, this time it's a class instance and a closure that are keeping each other alive.

```
class Automobile3
{
    let name : String
    init(name: String, owner: Person) {
        self.name = name
        self.owner = owner
    }

    lazy var information : () -> String = {
        if let driver = self.driver {
            return "Automobile \(self.name) is owned by \(self.owner) and driven by \
            (driver)"
        } else {
            return "Automobile \(self.name) is owned by \(self.owner) and driven by \
            (self.owner)"
        }
    }

    weak var driver : Person? = nil
    unowned var owner : Person
    deinit {
        println("Automobile \(name) is being deinitialized")
    }
}
```

This example shows how to create a strong reference cycle when using a closure. The class Automobile3 defines a lazy property called information, which combines various other properties and returns a string representation of the automobile. The property information is not a regular property; it's a function that takes no arguments and returns a string, () -> String, and I'm assigning a closure.

The class instance's information property holds a strong reference to the closure and the closure references self in its body. The closure captures itself, which means the closure has a strong reference to the instance of the class.

> **Note** Even though the closure references self multiple times, only one strong reference is captured.

To solve this problem, Swift provides a solution that uses a closure capture list, which defines the rules to use when capturing one or more reference types within the closure's body. As part of the definition of a closure, you can define how to capture the instances you need to use. Use either unowned or weak, depending how the instances are defined.

To define a capture list, put each reference to a class instance, together with either the weak or unowned keyword, in square brackets, before the implementation of the closure, like so:

```
{ [capture list] (arguments) -> returnType in
}
```

If you don't have any arguments or a return type for the closure, you can omit those and the syntax looks like this

```
{ [capture list] in
}
```

> **Note**   You want to capture self as unowned because it should never become nil.

Now that you know how to resolve a strong reference cycle, let's fix that in the example. The only thing I need to change is to add the capture list to the closure:

```
lazy var information : () -> String = {
    [unowned self] in
    if let driver = self.driver {
        return "Car \(self.name) is owned by \(self.owner) and driven by \(driver)"
    } else {
        return "Car \(self.name) is owned by \(self.owner) and driven by \(self.owner)"
    }
}
```

In this case, self is captured as an unowned reference, and the strong reference cycle is broken.

Summary

Managing memory in Swift is a complicated subject. You learned how Swift manages its memory using ARC. If you aren't careful how you define properties on the classes, it can lead to strong reference cycles.

You learned how to break those strong reference cycles, especially when it comes to closures. Even the simplest form of closure can cause a strong reference cycle, and you saw how to avoid those using a capture list.

Chapter 15

Protocols

In the real world, people on official business are often required to follow strict procedures when dealing with certain situations. Law enforcement officials, for example, are required to "follow protocol" when making inquiries or collecting evidence.

In the world of object-oriented programming, it's important to be able to define a set of behaviors that's expected of an object in a given situation. As an example, a table view expects to be able to communicate with a data source object in order to find out what it's required to display. This means the data source must be able to respond to the specific messages the table view might send.

Protocols define the interface—a blueprint of methods, properties, and other requirements for a specific task. The protocol does not actually implement the functionality itself, it only describes the implementation.

Any object that implements the requirements a protocol describes is said to **conform** to the protocol. A protocol can require a specific instance of the type to have:

- Properties
- Instance methods
- Type methods
- Operators
- Subscripts

Syntax

You define a protocol in the same way you define classes, structures, and enumeration types:

```
protocol SomeProtocol {
    // Your protocol requirements
}
```

Your protocol can also inherit from another protocol:

```
protocol SomeProtocol : NSObjectProtocol {
    // Your protocol requirements
}
```

In Objective-C you could have a protocol and class with the same name, such as class NSObject and protocol NSObject, but in Swift the names can't be the same. In the preceding example, the protocol inherits from NSObjectProtocol, which is the same as NSObject protocol in Objective-C.

When a type conforms to one or more protocols, you define that type by giving the list of protocols after the colon separator, and you can list multiple protocols using the comma separator:

```
struct SomeStruct : SomeProtocol, AnotherProtocol {
        // your implementation of structure
}
```

If your class has a parent class, you can list the protocols after the parent class:

```
class SomeClass : ParentClass, SomeProtocol, AnotherProtocol {
        // your implementation of class
}
```

Properties

Protocols can require the implementing type (or conforming type) to provide a property that can be either gettable (read-only) or settable and gettable (read-write). The protocol doesn't specify that the specific property has to be stored or computed; the implementing type can implement the property as it likes as long as it conforms to the protocol interface.

If the property is settable, it can't be either a constant stored or gettable computed property. Only gettable properties can be used to satisfy any requirements.

Property requirements are always defined as var, not let. You define the property as either read-only or read-write by adding either the get function or both get and set functions in braces after the type declaration.

```
protocol SomeProtocol {
    // Your protocol requirements
    var readwriteProperty : Int { set get}
    var readonlyProperty : Int { get }
}
```

To define a type property, you prefix the property with the class keyword, even when you use the protocol for structures and enumerations.

```
protocol AnotherProtocol {
    class var typeProperty : Int { get set }
}
struct SomeStruct : SomeProtocol, AnotherProtocol {
    var readwriteProperty : Int
    private(set) var readonlyProperty : Int
    static var typeProperty : Int {
        get {
        return 0
        }

        set {

        }
    }
}
```

That was a simple example showing how to conform a structure to your protocols. But it doesn't really help us; let's look at a concrete example of how this works:

```
protocol FullName {
    var fullName : String { get }
}

struct Person : FullName {
    var lastName : String
    var firstName : String
    var middleName : String?

    init (firstName : String, lastName : String) {
        self.lastName = lastName
        self.firstName = firstName
    }

    var fullName : String {
        return firstName + (middleName == nil ? "" : " " + middleName!) + " " + lastName
    }
}

var alan = Person(firstName: "Alan", lastName: "Turing")
println(alan.fullName)
alan.middleName = "Mathison"
println(alan.fullName)
```

Methods

The most common requirements for a protocol are specific instance and type methods. You define the methods in a protocol as you'd define them in a type but without the implementation, that is, without the curly braces.

> **Note** When defining a method requirement, you can't specify defaults values for method parameters.

Similar to the property requirement, you use the keyword `class` when defining type methods, even when they are implemented in structures and enumerations with the `static` keyword.

The following example shows a protocol that requires two methods, an instance method and a type method. Neither of these methods takes any arguments or has a return value.

```
protocol MethodProtocol {
    func instanceMethod ()
    class func typeMethod ()
}
```

If your methods will modify the state of a structure or enumeration type, you have to specify that with `mutating` keyword:

```
protocol MethodProtocol {
    mutating func instanceMethod ()
    class func typeMethod ()
}
```

Initializers

Protocols can require a specific initializer to be implemented by a conforming class. You define these initializers in the protocol just as with regular initializers, but without the curly braces.

```
protocol SomeProtocol {
    init(parameter : Double)
}
```

The conforming class can implement these as either convenience or designated initializers. In either case the implementation of the initializer must be marked using the `required` modifier.

```
class SomeClass : SomeProtocol {
    required init(parameter: Double) {
    }
}
```

The required modifier is necessary to ensure that the conforming class provides an explicit or inherited implementation of the initializer on all of its subclasses so they conform to the protocol as well.

> **Note**   You don't need to provide the `required` keyword for an initializer if the class is marked as `final`.

If the subclass overrides a designated initializer and also implements the matching initializer requirements from a protocol, then both the required and override keywords must be used to properly satisfy both requirements.

```
class ParentClass {
    init(parameter : Double) {
    }
}

class SomeClass : ParentClass, SomeProtocol {
    required override init(parameter: Double) {
    }
}
```

You can also require failable initializers in your protocol. A failable initializer requirement can be satisfied by either a failable or nonfailable initializer. For a nonfailable initializer, you can use a failable initializer and explicitly unwrap it.

Protocols as Types

When you define a protocol, it becomes a type that can be used much like any other type, even though the protocol doesn't provide its own implementation.

Protocol types can be used as:

- Parameter types for methods.

- Return types for methods.

- A type for a constant, variable or property.

- A type for an item in an array, dictionary, or other container.

    ```
    class SomeClass {
        var protocolConformingProperty : SomeProtocol
        init(someObject : SomeProtocol) {
            self.protocolConformingProperty = someObject
        }
    }
    var myClass = SomeClass (someObject: SomeStruct(readwriteProperty:
    5, readonlyProperty: 10))
    println(myClass.protocolConformingProperty.readonlyProperty)
    ```

In this example, SomeClass has a property that conforms to a protocol, and the init method has the object that the class is initialized with as the same protocol type.

Delegation

If you've been an iOS or OSX developer for any length of time, you've no doubt used tableviews, which have one property called delegate. Delegate is a design pattern that delegates or offloads some of the work to an instance of another type that's better suited to it.

The following example defines a simple protocol for a download manager. It defines two methods to start and end a download.

```
public protocol DownloadManagerDelegate : NSObjectProtocol {
    func downloadManagerDidStart(manager : DownloadManager)
    func downloadManagerDidEnd(manager : DownloadManager)
}

public class DownloadManager
{
    public weak var delegate : DownloadManagerDelegate?

    init() {
        println("init")
    }

    public func GET(path : String, parameters : [String : AnyObject]? = nil) {
        self.delegate?.downloadManagerDidStart(self)
        // do you work
        self.delegate?.downloadManagerDidEndself)
    }
}
```

My view controller will adopt the protocol to keep track of the start and end of the network calls I'll be making. To use it in my controller, I need to implement the required methods:

```
class ViewController: UIViewController, DownloadManagerDelegate
{
    private var downloadManager : DownloadManager?

    override func viewDidLoad() {
        super.viewDidLoad()
        // Do any additional setup after loading the view, typically from a nib.
        self.downloadManager = DownloadManager()
        self.downloadManager?.delegate = self

        self.downloadManager?.GET("/articles")
    }

    func downloadManagerDidStart(manager: DownloadManager) {
        println("Download did start.")
    }

    func downloadManagerDidEnd(manager: DownloadManager) {
        println("Download did finish.")
    }
}
```

Conformance with Extensions

If you have an existing type that you'd like to conform to a protocol, you can do that by implementing the protocol requirements in the extension.

Protocols and Collection Types

A protocol type can be a member of a collection type, such as an array or dictionary. As you know, once a protocol is defined it becomes a first-class type object, and you can simply use it in place of values:

```
let items[SomeProtocol] = [object1, object2, object3]
```

This example shows that items is a collection of objects that conform to SomeProtocol; this is one way to store heterogeneous objects. Objects don't have to be of the same type as long as they conform to the protocol you want.

Protocol Inheritance

Protocols can inherit from one or more parent protocols, as you saw with the DownloadManagerDelegate protocol that inherits from NSObjectProtocol. The syntax is similar to that of class inheritance, but allows listing of multiple parent protocols.

```
protocol SomeProtocol : ParentProtocol {
}

protocol SomeOtherProtocol : ParentProtocol, AnotherParentProtocol {
}
```

You can limit the protocol to be used with classes only, and not structures or enumerations, by adding the class keyword before the list of parent protocols. Both of the following examples limit the use MyProtocol to reference types and not value types:

```
protocol MyProtocol : class {
}
protocol MyProtocol : class, NSObjectProtocol {
}
```

Protocol Composition

Sometimes you want to be able to require a type to conform to multiple protocols. Swift provides a protocol composition construct that lets you do this. Instead of using the protocol type as the type of the variable, you replace it with a composition having the format protocol<SomeProtocol, AnotherProtocol>, which will create a temporary local protocol that combines all the listed protocols.

```
func myFunction(parameter : protocol <SomeProtocol, AnotherProtocol>) {
}
```

This function's parameter is required to conform to all of the protocols. In this case, if the instance of the type doesn't conform to both protocols it will be rejected.

Summary

In this chapter, I introduced the concept of protocols. You define a protocol by listing a set of methods inside a protocol block. Objects adopt this protocol by including the protocol name after the colon when defining a type. When an object adopts a formal protocol, it promises to implement every required method that's listed in the protocol. The compiler helps you keep your promise by giving you an error if you don't implement all the protocol's methods.

Chapter **16**

Generics

Generics are one of the most powerful aspects of the Swift language. If you are coming from Objective-C, this is a new concept, and it might take some getting used to. The main purpose of generics is to enable the writing of adaptable, reusable code.

Generic Functions

Let's take a look at a simple function that compares two integers. The function takes two arguments of type Int and returns a Boolean true if two values are the same.

```
func equalInts(a : Int, b : Int) -> Bool {
    return a == b
}
```

What if you want to compare two double values or strings? You have to write two new functions:

```
func equalDoubles(a : Double, b : Double) -> Bool {
    return a == b
}

func equalStings(a : String, b : String) -> Bool {
    return a == b
}
```

In all three functions, the body is identical. The only difference is the type of the arguments they take. It would be really useful, and more flexible, to write one function that could compare two values and return the proper result. Generics allow you to do that. Let's write a generic function that lets you compare any type and return the proper result.

To define a function that takes generic values you create a generic type, which will be replaced by the actual type when you use the function—you put the generic type at the end of the function name in angle brackets and replace the actual types with the generic types in the arguments.

```
func someFunction<T>(argument : T)
```

> **Note** I'll use T, short for type, for my generic type. You can use anything as long as it's not an existing type. Also, it's recommended that you use the same convention to name the types.

The preceding function definition tells the compiler that I have a placeholder type and the argument is of that type, and I'll replace the placeholder with the actual type every time this function is called.

When you call the function, you don't need to use the angle brackets:

```
var a : Int = 5
func someFunction(a)
```

The complier will infer the type of the placeholder to be the `Int` type. If I call this function with a type of `Double`, the compiler will infer the placeholder type to be `Double`.

To implement the values equal function, I simply replace the type with the generic:

```
func areValuesEqual<T>(a : T, b: T) -> Bool {
    return a == b
}
```

But I'm not quite done yet. If you try to implement it like this, the compiler will give you an error because the compiler doesn't know how to compare two generic types. It's easy to do that for `Int`, `Double,` and `String`, but what if you're using a custom type? You need to limit the function to any type that implements the `==` operator, which is defined in the `Equatable` protocol.

```
func areValuesEqual<T : Equatable>(a : T, b: T) -> Bool {
    return a == b
}
```

Now I'm set. I can tell if two instances of the object are the same as long as they implement the `Equatable` protocol. And I know that numeric and string types are equatable.

```
areValuesEqual(a, b)
areValuesEqual(b, c)

areValuesEqual1 , 1)
areValuesEqual(2.3, 2.4)
```

The generic type is not limited to arguments. It can also be a return type. And it can be used inside a function to declare new variables of the given type:

```
func areValuesEqual<T : Equatable>(a : T, b: T) -> Bool {
    var localVarible : T = a
    return localVarible == b
}

func someFunction<T>(values : [T]) -> T {
        // implementation
}
```

If you want two generic types of arguments, you can simply add another type to the list:

```
func someFunction<T1, T2>(t2 : T2, t1 : T1)
```

In the preceding example, I narrowed down the types the function can handle. This is called *type constraint*. The general form of type constraint is just adding the class or protocol name after the type, separated by colon:

```
func someFunction<Type1 : SomeClass, Type2 : SomeProtocol>(arugment1 : Type2, argument2 :
Type1) {
}
```

This function has two arguments, one of type SomeClass (or derived from it) and the other conforming to the protocol SomeProtocol.

Generic Types

In Chapter 10 I used a Stack type. The implementation only worked with the Double type. If I want to use it for some other type, I have to implement another version. Sometimes it's not possible to know the type of data you'll be using. Imagine a new data type that a user defined that would like to use my stack implementation. That's not possible, though, because I haven't provided an implementation for that type. Let's take a look at the original implementation.

```
struct DoubleStack {
    private var stack = [Double]()

    func empty () -> Bool {
        println("Stack Empty")
        return stack.count == 0
    }

    func peek () -> Double? {
        return stack.last
    }
```

```
    mutating func pop () -> Double? {
        let value = stack.last
        if nil != value {
            stack.removeLast()
        }
        return value
    }

    mutating func push (item : Double) {
        stack.append(item)
    }
}
```

Since this implementation works only with doubles, if I want to store other types I'd have to implement one for each of the types. Let's implement a generic version. The syntax is similar to the generic function:

```
struct Stack<T> {
    private var stack = [T]()

    func empty () -> Bool {
        println("Stack Empty")
        return stack.count == 0
    }

    func peek () -> T? {
        return stack.last
    }

    mutating func pop () -> T? {
        let value = stack.last
        if nil != value {
            stack.removeLast()
        }
        return value
    }

    mutating func push (item : T) {
        stack.append(item)
    }
}
```

The generic version is almost the same; I added the generic type to the name of the type. I replaced the Double type with my generic type. To use the generic type is a little different because the type can't be inferred. If I want to use the generic type for integers, I have to tell the compiler when I'm creating an instance of the stack, and I do that by replacing the generic type with the actual type.

```
var intStack = Stack<Int>()
var stringStack = Stack<String>()
```

The first example creates a stack of `Int` types and the second of `String` types. You can even create a stack for your own types if you want. In the following example, I create a new type called `MyClass,` which lets me create a stack that will hold instances of my new type.

```
class MyClass {
}

var myClassStack = Stack<MyClass>()
```

Associated Types

If you want to define a protocol that needs to use a generic type, you might assume you could do something like this:

```
protocol SomeProtocol<T> {
}
```

You can't, but there is a solution. It's called an *associated type*. An associated type gives a placeholder name (or alias) to a type that's used as part of a protocol. That type will not be defined until the protocol is adopted.   To do this you use the `typealias` keyword:

```
protocol SomeProtocol {
        typealias GenericType
}
```

In this example, I define an associated type called `GenericType`. Now I can use this where I need an actual type. If I were to add a function requirement for this protocol that took an argument whose type will be defined when the protocol is adopted, I'd write it as:

```
protocol SomeProtocol {
    typealias GenericType
    func someFunction(argument : GenericType)
}
```

And when a type adopts the protocol, it has to set the type of the generic type:

```
class SomeClass : SomeProtocol {
    typealias GenericType = Int
    func someFunction(argument: GenericType) {
        // do your processing
    }
}
```

The class `SomeClass` will adopt the protocol. The first thing I do is set the type of the `GenericType` by defining it as an `Int`. Now, in the class where `GenericType` is used, the compiler will substitute `Int` for it.

Because Swift has type inference, I don't need to explicitly tell the compiler what GenericType is if I just use Int instead of GenericType as the argument type for someFunction.

```
class SomeClass : SomeProtocol {
    func someFunction(argument: Int) {
        // do your processing
    }
}
```

Now I'll create a protocol called Collection, which I can use for arrays, lists, stacks or any kind of collection. What is common for these types?

- The number of items in the collection

- Adding an item to the collection

- Getting an item from the collection

Using an associated type, I can define a generic protocol to have three functions that might look like this:

```
protocol Collection {
    typealias CollectionType
    func count() -> Int
    mutating func add(item : CollectionType)
    subscript(index : Int) -> CollectionType { get }
}
```

The following shows what the new version of the stack type would look like. I don't have to explicitly state the type for the Collection protocol; it is inferred by the type system from the add function.

```
struct Stack<T> : Collection {
    private var stack = [T]()

    func empty () -> Bool {
        println("Stack Empty")
        return stack.count == 0
    }

    func peek () -> T? {
        return stack.last
    }

    mutating func pop () -> T? {
        let value = stack.last
        if nil != value {
            stack.removeLast()
        }
        return value
    }
```

```
    mutating func push (item : T) {
        stack.append(item)
    }

    // MARK - Collection Protocol
    func count() -> Int {
        return self.stack.count
    }

    mutating func add(item: T) {
        self.push(item)
    }

    subscript(index : Int) -> T {
        return self.stack[index]
    }
}
```

Suppose you want to compare two collections and see if the items in the collection are the same. If you have two stack types, you could write an operator on the type and simply compare those. What if you have two different types, a stack and a list, both of which conform to the Collection protocol? You'd have to write an operator for stack that compares against a list, and you'd also have to write an operator on the list type that would compare against the stack type. That's lots of duplicate code. Moreover, if you decide to write another type that also conforms to the Collection protocol, you then have to write the same code for every type you use. That would produce an exponentially large set of duplicate code. The best approach is to write a global function that take two collection types, compare them, and returns a true or false.

```
func areIdentical<T1 : Collection, T2 : Collection>(collection1 : T1, collection2 : T2) ->
Bool
```

To implement this function and have it return the correct result involves certain requirements:

1. T1 and T2 must conform to the Collection protocol.

2. Types in the collection must be the same.

3. Types must be comparable.

4. There must be the same number of items.

5. Each item must be in the same order.

You could just implement the method and check for items at runtime, but what if you could do that at compile time? Swift provides a mechanism called a where clause. When you define a function, you put the where clause after the type requirements. The general form is, just like with types, each clause is separated by a comma:

```
func myFunction<Type1, Type1 where Clause1, Clause2> (arguments) -> ReturnType
```

Here's the updated function definition:

```
func areIdentical<T1 : Collection, T2 : Collection
    where T1.CollectionType == T2.CollectionType, T1.CollectionType : Equatable>
    (collection1 : T1, collection2 : T2) -> Bool
```

The first clause enforces that types of the collection must be the same, and the second clause enforces that T1 must conform to Equatable protocol, which in turn enforces that T2 must also be equatable.

Now the implementation of the function becomes really easy—all I have to do is make sure that the number of items are the same and that each item is the same.

Summary

Whoa, that's lots of new stuff. Generics are one of the features that make Swift a very powerful language and a big departure from Objective-C. In Objective-C, all objects are derived from a single base class called NSObject, so every object is of type NSObject. In Swift, you can have objects that don't have parent classes, which brings about the need for generics. Now you can write less code by making your code generic, and that, in turn, means fewer bugs.

Chapter 17

Expressions

Expressions are the building blocks of any program. Values, variables, constants, and functions are combined to form expressions, which, in turn, are combined to form a program. When the program is run, expressions are interpreted according to the rules set by the particular language. These rules can include precedence and associativity, and they produce results and possibly a new state for the program.

Swift is no different. It provides four types of expressions:

- Primary
- Prefix
- Binary
- Postfix

Evaluating expressions in Swift produces a result, a side effect, or both. There are some expressions that require more information. I'll take a look at these and expand on their features and requirements.

> **Note** An expression is said to have a side effect if it modifies some state or has an observable interaction beyond the value of the expression.

Primary Expressions

Primary expressions are the simplest of the expressions. They provide access to values such as x, "This", 4.5, and so forth. These expressions are used in combination with operators to form compound expressions. Some are literal expressions, such as a string literal or a number literal. Other literal expressions are dictionaries and arrays, and the following built-in literals:

- __FILE__ is the name of the file that uses it, and it's a string.
- __LINE__ is the number of the line where it appears, and it's an Int.
- __COLUMN__ is the number of the column where it appears, and it's an Int.
- __FUNCTION__ is the name of the declaration in which it's used, and it's a String.

Prefix Expressions

A prefix expression, as the name implies, adds an operator to the beginning of a given expression. Prefix operators take one argument and have the general form:

```
prefix-operator right-hand-side
```

```
++index
-5
+192.983
```

Postfix Expressions

A postfix expression is where the operator is at the end. In Swift you have two-postfix expression:

- ++ increment
- -- decrement

To use thse you simply add them at the end of the number. 3++ or 3--

> **Note**   Technically all primary expression are also postfix expressions.

Binary Expressions

Binary expressions are the most common in most languages. They take an argument on the left-hand side (lhs), then an infix operator, and another argument on the right-hand side (rhs). The arguments can be either an expression or an instance of a type, depending on the operator.

```
left-hand-side infix-operator right-hand-side
```

Swift provides a very rich set of binary operators, the most common of these binary expression is the assignment expression using the = operator.

Assignment Operator

The general form of the assignment operator is:

```
left-hand-side = right-hand-side
```

The lhs is an expression that will be assigned the value(s) from the rhs values. The lhs can be a simple value or a compound, such as a structure or an enumeration type. What's new with Swift is the tuple assignment—you can assign multiple values using a tuple. The one requirement is that the lhs tuple and the rhs tuple have the same structure. Here are some valid tuple assignments:

```
(a, b) = (4, 6.5)
(lastName, firstName, middleName) = ("Babbage", "Charles", nil)
(a, _, b, (c, d), x) = (5.0, "Hello", (6, "yellow"), "Apple")
```

If you want to ignore a value during an assignment, use the _ (underscore) in place of that part of the expression. In the third example, the value "Hello" is being ignored during the assignment.

Here are some invalid tuple assignments:

```
(a, b) = 5
(a, b) = (5)
(a, (b, c)) = (1, 2, 3)
```

Ternary Conditional

There's another infix operator that's not binary. It's called the ternary conditional operator and it requires three items. The operator looks like this ?: and works like an if-else statement but condensed to one line.

```
if condition {
        evaluate true
} else {
        evaluate false
}
```

With the ternary operator, you can rewrite that code as:

```
condition ? evaluate true : evaluate false
```

If-else statements don't return a value, but the ternary operation returns the value of the expression evaluated.

Casting Operators

Swift provides three operators to use when downcasting or introspection types.

- is, to check if the type is of a specific type.

- as, to downcast the type to another type.

- as?, to downcast as an optional type.

To check whether a type can be converted, simply use *expression* is *type*. The expression will return true if the expression evaluates to type, or false if expression doesn't evaluate to type.

The general form of these expressions is:

- Expression is type

- Expression as type

- Expression as? type1

To actually downcast the value, you can use either as or as?. The first is a forced unboxed cast. If the cast fails, you get a runtime error. With the second, if the downcast succeeds, it's wrapped in an optional. If it fails, the value is nil.

If the compiler knows at compile time that a type can't be cast, that results in a compile-time error. In Cocoa Touch frameworks you can always downcast to NSObject because all objects have the same root class. But in Swift, that's not the case, so if the class is not a subclass of another, casting isn't possible and the compiler will give an error.

Self and Super

There are two special expression types called self and super.

If used within the class function, the self expression refers to the type itself, but in an instance method it refers to a specific instance of that type. Self can be used in various forms:

```
self.type-member
self[subscript-index]
self(initializer-arguments)
self.init(initializer-arguments)
```

One special case is in mutating structures where you can assign a new value to self.

Super is used when referring to a superclass. If the type has a superclass, the form is as follows:

```
super.type-member
super[subscript-index]
super.init(initlizer-arguments)
```

You can also use `self` as a postfix expression to get the name of the type.

```
expression.self
type.self
```

The first example returns the instance of the expression: A.self just refers to a. The second one returns the type.

Closures and Functions

You already know that functions are just named closures, but the syntax is different and takes getting used to.

Closures

Closures create a block of code that can be passed as a type. The general syntax is:

```
{ (closure arguments) -> return-type in
      closure-body
}
```

If you don't have arguments or a return type, these can be inferred. There are special forms of closures. Here are rules you can apply to make your closure as verbose or terse as you'd like.

- A closure can omit the types of its arguments.

- A closure can omit its return type.

- If you omit both the argument types and names, omit the `in` keyword before the statements.

- If you omit the argument list, the arguments are explicitly named $0, $1, ...

- If the closure has only a single expression in the body, this implies that the closure returns the value of the expression; the return statement can be omitted.

Here are some examples; these are all equivalent:

```
{ (a : Int, b : Int) -> Int in
    return a % b
}

{ (a, b) in
    return a % b
}

{ return $0 % %1 }

{ $0 % %1 }
```

If you use a reference type within the closure, you'll be capturing the variable strongly, as I discussed in Chapter 14.

If you specify a capture list, you have to specify the in keyword in the closure.

```
{ self.type-member } // strong reference to self
{ [weak self] in self!.type-member } // weak reference to self
{ [unowned self] in self.type-member } // unowned reference
{ [weak weakSelf = self] in weakSelf!.type-member }
```

Function Calls

To call a function, the syntax is the name of the function followed by a list of arguments in parentheses separated by commas:

```
function-name(argument1, argument2)
```

If the function call requires argument names, you add the argument names before each argument, separated by a colon:

```
function-name(argumentName1 : argument1, argumentName2 : argument2)
```

There's a special case where, if the function has a trailing closure (a final argument), you can move the closure out from the argument list and add it to the end of the function call:

```
function-name(argument1, {closure})
function-name(argument1) {closure}
```

Both of these statements are equivalent. If the closure is the only argument, you can even skip the parentheses

```
Function-name({closure})
Function-name{closure}
```

There's also a special initializer function called init:

```
expression.init(argument-list)
```

You can't use the init functions to initialize variables since they don't return any value:

```
var result = type.classFunction //correct
var result = type.init // error
```

Implicit Member Expression

In previous examples I used explicit .type-member expressions. When the type can be inferred, you can use an abbreviated form for enumeration cases or class methods. Inside the classes you don't need the dot syntax to access methods, initializers, and so forth. The only time you have to be explicit is when the name of an argument to a method is the same as the property name.

```
var domainMask : NSSearchPathDomainMask = .UserDomainMask
```

With explicit member expression, in contrast, you explicitly access the value:

```
var instance = SomeClass()
instance.member-item
```

For tuples, the member items are accessed by numeric dereference:

```
var myTuple = (a, b, c, d)
myTuple.1 // returns b
```

Optionals

One of the features of Swift is the optional type. When you declare an optional variable, you are telling the compiler that this variable might or might not have a value. To get a valid value from an optional is called *unwrapping* the optional.

If you know that the value of an optional is not nil, you can force the unwrapping using the ! (bang) operator. If the value that's unwrapped is not a valid value, you get a runtime error.

```
var a : Int? = 0
var b : Int = 5
a! += b
```

If you want to be safe, you can use optional chaining to unwrap optionals. With optional chaining you conditionally unwrap the optional to see if it contains a value, and if it does the expression is evaluated; if not, nil is returned. The return value from optional chaining is always an optional. The syntax is similar to the forced unwrap but uses ? instead of !.

```
expression?
```

This expression returns the value as an optional. This is good, but it really works well if you chain optionals to evaluate. The way it works is that if the optional unwraps as a valid value, the rest of the expression is evaluated and the result is returned, otherwise nil is returned.

```
class SomeClass {
        func someFunction() -> Int {
                return 42
        }
}

var someInstance : SomeClass?
var result = someInstance?.someFunction()
```

The type of the result is Int? because even though the return type of someFunction is Int, someInstance is an optional. If someInstance exists, the result will have the value 42; if someInstance is nil then result will be nil.

There is another way to optionally unwrap an optional using the if-let expression.

```
if let unwrapped = someInstance {
        result = unwrapped.someFunction()
}
```

In this case, if someInstance has a valid value, it is assigned to unwrapped and then the if statement is evaluated to be true and the statements in the if statement are executed, otherwise the condition for the if statement is evaluated to be false and it's skipped.

Summary

This was a quick overview of expressions; there's a lot more to learn and experiment with. You'll be using most if not all of these expressions in your programs.

Chapter 18

Interoperability with Objective-C

Swift is an awesome language and works great by itself, but when you're writing iOS or OSX applications, you have to interface with the frameworks that Apple provides and perhaps with your own existing frameworks. You may be able to rewrite your frameworks in Swift, but Apple hasn't provided its frameworks in Swift yet, if it ever will. Apple does provide interoperability with existing frameworks that use the Objective-C and C APIs.

> **Note** Interoperability in this case is the capability of interaction between the Swift and Objective-C APIs in either direction. This means being able to use the Swift API in Objective-C code and the Objective-C API in Swift code.

To use Swift in Objective-C or vice versa, you need to set up the project so you can mix and match these languages properly. Let's start by creating a new Swift project. Start Xcode if you haven't already started it. You can select the new project either from the welcome window or from File ➤ New ➤ Project…(⇧⌘N). I'm going to start with an iOS single view application.

Once you've selected the project, click the Next button to get the Project settings window (Figure 18-1). Enter the project name and make sure to select Swift as the language. Now you're ready to experiment.

Choose options for your new project:

Product Name:	Explore
Organization Name:	Apress, Inc.
Organization Identifier:	com.apress
Bundle Identifier:	com.apress.Explore
Language:	Swift
Devices:	iPhone
	☐ Use Core Data

Cancel   Previous   Next

Figure 18-1. *Project settings window*

If you look at the project explorer, you'll see a couple of Swift files already in your project. Let's look at the `ViewController.swift` file.

> **Note**   Unlike Objective-C/C/C++, Swift doesn't use header files; the implementation and interface reside in the dot swift file.

After the comments in the file you'll see the `import UIKit` declaration, which tells the Swift compiler you'd like to use the UIKit framework. In Objective-C you'd use either `#import <UIKit/UIKit.h>` or `@import UIKit;` to accomplish the same thing.

Import Process

The Swift compiler will look at the header files, compile them into Objective-C modules, and import them as native Swift APIs. The import process determines how the APIs (functions, classes, methods, and types) declared in Objective-C appear in Swift. This process will remap:

- Objective-C types to equivalent Swift types.
- Certain Objective-C types to Swift native types, such as `NSArray` to `Array`, or `NSString` to `String`.
- Certain Objective-C concepts to equivalent Swift concepts.

> **Note** You can't import C++ code directly into Swift, you have to export your code wrapped in an Objective-C interface.

The process of importing Swift code into Objective-C works similarly.

Interoperability

What happens when you import Objective-C code into Swift? First, pointers are mapped to Swift optionals. So

```
NSString *myString = nil
```

will be imported as:

```
var myString : NSString? = nil;
```

Actually, that's not strictly true. The second thing that happens is that certain types, such as NSString, are mapped to native Swift objects such as String, so the actual mapping is:

```
var myString : String? = nil;
```

The Objective-C type id is mapped to the Swift AnyObject protocol. This protocol can represent an instance of any object type, just as id represents any object in Objective-C.

```
id myObject = nil;
var myObject : AnyObject? = nil
var myObject1 : AnyObject = NSString()
```

> **Note** The AnyObject protocol represents a safe object. If you'd like to be able to assign a nil value, it has to be boxed in an optional.

Keep in mind that, in Swift, once a variable is assigned a type, you can't change the type of that variable. AnyObject is different, however. It can hold different types of objects.

```
var myObject : AnyObject = NSString()
myObject = NSArray()
```

Since AnyObject does not represent a specific type, you are allowed to call any Objective-C method or access any property without having to cast the type to specific class.

```
var myObject : AnyObject = UIView(frame: CGRectZero)
var myView = UIView()
myObject.addSubview(myView)
```

The types of objects are determined at runtime in Objective-C, and that's also true for AnyObject: Its type is determined at runtime. Because of this, it's possible to write unsafe code. If you try to call a method or access a property that doesn't exist for a type, this will cause a runtime error similar to Objective-C. Let's say you try to call a method from NSArray, such as objectAtIndex(0):

```
var myObject : AnyObject = UIView(frame: CGRectZero)
let myValue = myObject.objectAtIndex(0)
```

There's no syntax error, but you'll get an error at runtime because the method objectAtIndex doesn't exist for UIView. If you run this program, you'll get a runtime error and crash the program. The error message will say, "unrecognized selector sent to instance," which is an Objective-C runtime telling you method you're trying to call on an object doesn't exist.

You can work around this problem by using optionals. What's really happening in the preceding code is something like this:

```
myObject.objectAtIndex!(0)
```

Notice the implicit unwrapping operation. You can rewrite that code with an optional:

```
let myValue : AnyObject? = myObject.objectAtIndex?(0)
```

Now the code won't cause the runtime error and crash the program when the objectAtIndex method doesn't exist as the runtime will check that and set the value to nil.

Since a method call on AnyObject may or may not succeed, that value is returned as the optional AnyObject? type. Before using it, you should check type of the resulting value.

Let's say the call succeeds and you get some instance of an object. You should check the type:

```
if let myImage = myValue as? UIImage {
    // do something with image
}
```

Here I'm checking if the instance returned is of type UIImage. If that's true, I assign it to myImage and then I can safely use it in my code.

Object Initialization

Swift will import the init methods from Objective-C with the new Swift syntax; the regular - (instancetype)init will be imported as init(). If you have been a good Objective-C citizen and named your init methods that take arguments with initWithSomething:(Type *)type, those methods will be imported with following transformations:

- The methods will be named init.
- The string With will be dropped.
- In the remaining string (<Something>), the first letter will be lowercased and that string will become the name of the first argument.
- Any other arguments that exist will be added.

Here's what my fictional example looks like:

```
init(something : Type)
```

Let's take a look at a concrete example.

```
- (instancetype)initWithNibName:(NSString *)nibNameOrNil bundle:(NSBundle *)nibBundleOrNil;
```

will be mapped to

```
init(nibName nibNameOrNil: String?, bundle nibBundleOrNil: NSBundle?)
```

When creating an object, you don't need to call `alloc`; that's done implicitly for you:

```
UIViewController *controller = [[UIViewController alloc] initWithNibName:nil bundle:nil];

let viewController = UIViewController(nibName: nil, bundle: nil)
```

Notice that I don't explicitly call the `init` method. `UIViewController.init(...)` is a syntax error; Swift will match the correct `init` method based the arguments.

Factory methods for a type are also brought over with the same syntax as convenience `init` methods:

```
UIColor *color = [UIColor colorWithWhite:1.0f alpha:0.5f];
let color = UIColor(white: 1.0, alpha: 0.5)
```

Failable Initializers

In Objective-C, initializers explicitly return the object that was created. If the object creation fails, the initializer returns nil to tell the calling code that it has failed. In Swift, this pattern is called *failable initializers*. You name the failable initializer with an optional, so your init method name becomes `init?(...)`, which tells the compiler that this `init` method may fail and will return a `nil` if it does.

```
NSArray *array = [NSArray arrayWithContentsOfFile:@"/tmp/myArray.plist"];
```

This call to create an array from a file can fail. It might fail if the file doesn't exist or if it can't be parsed into an array. The initializer will be imported as

```
convenience init?(contentsOfFile path: String)
```

Properties

To access Objective-C properties in Swift, you use the familiar dot syntax:

```
let view = UIView(frame: CGRectZero)
view.hidden = false
view.backgroundColor = UIColor.whiteColor()
```

I accessed two properties of view; one takes a simple Boolean value and the other takes a UIColor instance.

One thing to notice is that `whiteColor` is not a property. Because it has parentheses, it's a function. In Objective-C, properties are a user-level interface; the compiler generates methods, so when you are accessing properties you are actually calling methods without any arguments. Why is this distinction important? Because Swift will only import properties from Objective-C as properties if they are declared using the `@property` syntax; otherwise they will be imported as methods.

Methods

As you've seen in previous chapters, to call methods in Swift you use the dot syntax similar to properties. When importing methods into Swift, they get mapped to the Swift method syntax:

- The Swift function name derives from the first part of the Objective-C method name.

- The first argument is mapped as an unnamed argument.

- The rest of the arguments are mapped with names.

For example,

```
[collectionView dequeueReusableCellWithReuseIdentifier:CellIdentifier
forIndexPath:indexPath];
```

will become

```
collectionView.dequeueReusableCellWithReuseIdentifier(CellIdentifier, forIndexPath:
indexPath)
```

Blocks

Objective-C blocks are imported as closures. In Objective-C you define a block variable using the syntax:

```
void (^myBlockVariable)(BOOL finished, NSString *result) = ^(BOOL finished, NSString *result) {
// Block implementation
}
```

This block is named `myBlockVariable`, takes two arguments, and returns no results. In Swift, it would look like:

```
let myBlockVariable : (Bool, String) -> Void = {finished, result in
// Block implementation
}
```

The syntax may look different but they are compatible, which means when a method is expecting a block as an argument, you can pass a closure as a value. There are some differences, however.

Since Swift functions are named closures, you can pass a function in place of a closure as long as the types match, meaning the argument list and the return type are the same.

Closures capture variables the same way as blocks, but with one difference. In Objective-C blocks, the variables are copied and are immutable. In Swift, they are mutable and you use the __block keyword for the captured variables.

Object Comparison

When comparing objects, you can compare two properties. The first type of comparison is if two objects are pointing to the same instance of a type:

```
NSObject *myObject = [[NSObject alloc] init];
NSObject *anotherObject = myObject;
```

Both of these objects point to the exact same instance of NSObject. In Objective-C you compare two objects using the isEqual: method from the NSObject.

```
BOOL equal = [myObject isEqual:anotherObject];
```

In Swift you use the identity operator, === (three equal signs).

The other type of comparison is where two objects point to two different objects but have the same contents:

```
NSString *myString = @"My String";
NSString *anotherString = @"My String";
```

Even though they have the same content, and despite the fact they point to two different objects, this is called equality. In Objective-C you use the isEqualToString: method to compare if two strings are same. In Swift you use the equal to operator, == (two equal signs), to determine whether the contents of the objects are same.

If you derive a Swift class from an NSObject, Swift will implement the == operator and call the isEqual: method. So you should implement this method in your Swift subclasses. If you don't derive a Swift class from NSObject and you try to use the isEqual: method in Objective-C, you'll get a runtime error so make sure to implement the isEqual: method.

Type Compatibility

Objective-C uses a dynamic runtime while Swift uses both dynamic and not dynamic runtimes, depending on how the type is defined. If the type is derived from:

An Objective-C class, then Swift uses a dynamic runtime. Otherwise, it doesn't use a dynamic runtime unless you specifically tell it that a dynamic runtime is needed.

When importing Objective-C into Swift, you don't have to do anything specific. You have access to all the properties, methods, and so on.

When exposing Swift classes to Objective-C, you can control how they are exposed. In Swift you can have classes that inherit from Objective-C-based classes such as NSObject, or those that are purely Swift classes.

If you inherit a Swift class from an Objective-C class, all of its properties, methods, subscripts, and initializers become available to other Objective-C classes.

If you have a class that doesn't inherit from Objective-C, use the @objc keyword before the class definition to make it available:

```
@objc public class MyClass {
}
```

This will cause the class to be available to Objective-C classes. You can also add the @objc attribute to any method, initializer, subscript, or property to make it available to the runtime.

In the example, I added the attribute to my class. The compiler will take that hint and add the @objc attribute to every non-private method, property, subscript, and initializer.

If you use the other keywords, such as @IBOutlet, @IBAction and @NSManaged, the @objc attribute is automatically added.

When exporting Swift methods to Objective-C, the compiler will map the method names correctly to their Objective-C equivalents:

```
func myFunction(argument1 : ArgumentType) -> ReturnType
```

This method will be translated to

```
- (ReturnType)myFunction:(ArgumentType *)argument1
```

The exception to this rule is the initializer method. By default, initWith is added to the beginning of the name init. So (myArgument : ArgumentType) will be translated to - (instancetype)initWithMyArgument:(ArgumentType *)myArgument.

Remember that Swift can use the full set of UNICODE characters for its names, including class name, methods, properties, and so forth. Also, Swift uses namespaces and prepends the module name to the class names. If you have a class called MyClass in your application named MyApplication (which is a module), the full name of the class would be MyApplication.MyClass. To work around these issues, the @objc attribute has an extended form where you specify the Objective-C names. In Swift you can have a class named 🐶🐮, but in Objective-C this would cause a compile-time error. You can give an explicit Objective-C name using @objc(DogCow). This also removes the namespaces. Even if the name of your class is not in non-ASCII characters but you just want to remove the namespaces, you need to do this:

```
@objc(DogCow)
public class 🐶🐮 {
}
```

You can also do the same with method names. For example, func ∑ (array : [Double]) -> Double needs to be rewritten so Objective-C can correctly use the method:

```
@objc(sum:)
func ∑(array : [Double]) -> Double
```

Dynamic Dispatch

Even after adding the @objc attribute to your methods, there's still no guarantee of using dynamic dispatch. The compiler can optimize the code at will for performance and skip the dynamic dispatch. Typically, you don't need to worry about this, but sometimes you need to have that certainty that the method or property will be called using the dynamic dispatch system.

You use the keyword dynamic to force the dynamic dispatch, usually in the case of key-value-observation (KVO), or if you want to switch method implementations at runtime:

```
dynamic public func myFunction() -> Void
```

Selectors

In Objective-C you can create a selector object (SEL) using the @selector(nameOfSelector) that can be assigned as an action. The SEL object is imported to Swift as a Selector type.

```
SEL mySelector = @selector(mySelector:);
var mySelector : Selector = "mySelector:"
```

You will notice that I just assigned a string literal to the selector type, because a string literal can be converted to a Selector type. So you don't have to explicitly create a Selector object; you can just use a string literal where a selector is required as an argument.

```
let barButtonItem = UIBarButtonItem(barButtonSystemItem: .Done, target: self, action: "done:")
```

> **Note**   The performSelector class of methods is not imported into Swift because of safety reasons.

Property Attributes

Some of the attributes that were used when defining properties will be used and others will be discarded. The default behavior for a property in Swift is strong. In Objective-C it's assigned; weak has the same meaning in both Swift and Objective-C. There are no read-write or read-only attributes. You define those by using either the let and var keywords or by providing either getter only or getter and setter.

The copy attribute is translated to the @NSCopying protocol so the type must conform to that protocol. There is no @dynamic keyword needed. This was a key requirement for Core Data objects; for that, the @NSManaged keyword is provided.

Namespaces and Class

I've already talked about namespaces and how the names of Swift classes have module names prepended to them. One solution is to export them using the @objc(name) to give an Objective-C compatible name.

If you don't want to do that, you can use the fully qualified names when using those classes. If the class is in a framework called MySuperFramework, you'd use the class name MySuperFramework.ClassName. Even if you don't have a framework, your application is a namespace. If the application name is MyApplication, the fully qualified name is MyApplication.ClassName. Any time you have to use a string for a name, such as NSClassFromString, you'll need to provide a fully qualified name:

```
Class class = NSClassFromString(@"MyApplication.ClassName")
```

When you work with Core Data objects, the interface expects names without namespaces. In the editor, where you specify the name of the class for an entity, you need to provide fully qualified name.

Cocoa Data Types

Swift will automatically map some of the foundation types to native Swift types, as shown in Table 18-1.

Table 18-1. Swift foundation types mapped to native Swift types

Foundation Types	Swift Types
NSString, NSMutableString	String
NSArray, NSMutableArray	[AnyObject], Array<AnyObject>
NSDictionary, NSMutableDictionary	[NSObject : AnyObject]. Dictionary<NSObject, AnyObject>
NSNumber	Int, UInt. ...

Foundation Functions

Most of the Foundation functions will be imported into Swift, such as NSLog. On the other hand, NSAssert functions do not carry over. Use the native assert function instead.

Core Foundation

Core Foundation data types are automatically imported as Swift classes. For any Core Foundation functions that provide memory annotation, such as CF_RETURNS_RETAINED or CF_RETURNS_NOT_RETAINED, the memory is automatically managed. You don't have to call the CFRetain, CFRelease, or CFAutorelease functions, even when you create those objects.

When Swift imports Core Foundation types, the names get changed and the Ref suffix is dropped. For example, CFArrayRef will be imported as CFArray. One exception, CFTypeRef is completely mapped to AnyObject. Anywhere you use CFTypeRef you can now use AnyObject.

Any functions that are annotated with memory management where the compiler can't automatically manage the memory for those Core Foundation types, they are returned wrapped in the Unmanaged<T> structure. In that case you have to use a couple of functions to unwrap those to objects whose memory can be managed. These functions will convert an unmanaged object to a managed object.

- takeUnretainedValue: This function will return the wrapped object as unretained.

- takeRetainedValue: This function will return the wrapped object as retained.

In the following function I haven't defined how the memory is managed:

```
CFStringRef MyStringManipulationFunction(CFStringRef string)
```

This function will be imported as:

```
func MyStringManipulationFunction(string : CFString!)  -> Unmanaged<CFString>!
```

To unbox and have Swift manage the memory, I use:

```
var myResult = MyStringManipulationFunction(string).takeUnretainedValue()
```

Interacting with C

Objective-C is a superset of C, which means everything that C provides is also brought into Swift because it is part of Objective-C. The C primitive types are mapped as shown in Table 18-2.

Table 18-2. *C primitive types mapped*

C Type	Swift Type
int, short, long	CInt, CShort, CLong
Bool	CBool
unsigned int , unsigned short, unsigned long	CUnsignedInt, CUnsignedShort, CUnsignedLong
char, signed char	CChar
unsigned char	CUnsignedChar
float, double	CFloat, CDouble
wchar_t, char16_t, char32_t	CWideChar, CChar16, CChar32

Even though Swift will import these data types, it's recommended you use Swift native equivalent types.

Keep in mind as well that global constants are imported as Swift constants and simple macros are imported as Swift constants. For example, #define MY_PI 3.14 will be imported as let MY_PI = 3.14. Complex macros are not brought over.

Summary

Even though Swift is a new language with a new syntax and runtime, it still works with the existing Objective-C API. There are pain points because Swift is trying to do Objective-C without the bad parts and, for some time, we'll still have to deal with the existing code base. Pay close attention to the translation layer and to how the two-way bridge works. For now, it's recommended that you be verbose as to how you'd like to exchange APIs between Objective-C and Swift.

Chapter 19

Mix and Match

Whether you've decided to start a new project that uses Swift, or want to update an existing Objective-C project to use Swift, you'll end up needing both languages in your projects. Apple calls this feature *mix and match*, where code written in either language can co-exist and work with the other.

Xcode has made the process of working in a mix-and-match environment quite easy. You simply create the files you need and Xcode will prompt you with the appropriate actions to take.

You start with couple of important header files. The first is the bridging header where you define the Objective-C API you need to expose to Swift source files. And the other is the reverse bridging header, which the compiler generates and will be imported to Objective-C sources. The diagram of this process in Figure 19-1 makes the process look complex, but Xcode makes most of this transparent.

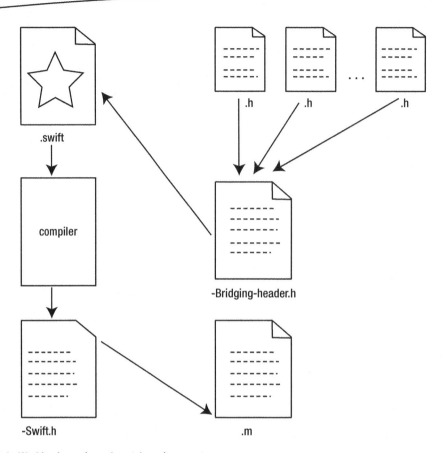

Figure 19-1. *Working in a mix-and-match environment*

The process does differ depending on whether you're using frameworks (modules) or putting everything in the main project.

Importing Objective-C into Swift in the Same App Target

To import Objective-C into Swift, the compiler needs a bridging header file. The first time you try to add Objective-C into a Swift project or Swift into an Objective-C project, Xcode will prompt you to add this file, as shown in Figure 19-2.

Figure 19-2. *Importing Objective-C into Swift*

If you accept the recommendation, Xcode will create a file named `<ProjectName>-Bridging-Header.h` file. If your project is named MyApp, for example, the header file will be called `MyApp-Bridging-Header.h`.

Note   Any dots (.) in your project name will be replaced with an underscore (_).

If you don't want Xcode to create a bridging header, you can create one yourself and tell Xcode to use it. To create a new header file, select the File ➤ New ➤ File... menu option, and select either the iOS or OS X template for Source ➤ Header File (Figure 19-3).

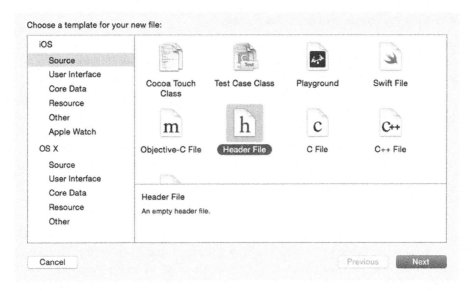

Figure 19-3. *Creating a header manually*

Once you've created the header manually, you need to tell Xcode you want to use it as the bridging header. You need to change the build settings for the project. Select your project and then the target.

From the target page, select the Build Settings option. In Build Settings, you'll see the filter search field at the top right of the pane. Type `bridging`, and Xcode will filter any setting that has the string `bridg`. The setting you're looking for is `Objective-C Bridging Header` (Figure 19-4).

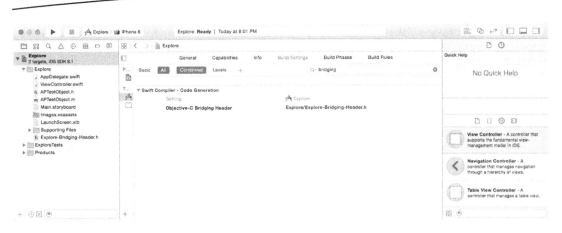

Figure 19-4. *Selecting the Objective-C Bridging Header string*

This is where you set the path to the Objective-C Bridging Header setting
(SWIFT_OBJC_BRIDGING_HEADER). This path is relative to your project.

Once the bridging header value is set, you can import all the Objective-C header files
needed for the APIs exposed to Swift.

```
//
//  Use this file to import your target's public headers that you would like to expose to Swift.
//

#import "APTestObject.h"
```

After you've added the Objective-C header files to your bridging header, the Objective-C
functionality will be available to all your Swift files without having to import anything in the
Swift files. In your Swift files, to create a new instance of an object, you simply use the Swift
syntax like this:

```
let myTestObject = APTestObject()
```

Importing Swift into Objective-C in the Same App Target

When you import a Swift project into Objective-C, you don't need to create any header
file. Xcode will automatically generate a one for you. The compiler-generated header file is
named after the name of the module it's defined in, <MyModule>-Swift.h, for example. You
can then import this umbrella header into your Objective-C files and use Swift functionality.

This generated header file will list all the interfaces marked with the public attribute. If the
application target has a bridging header, the interfaces marked as internal will be listed as
well. Any interfaces marked private will not be listed, unless you marked those interfaces
with the Objective-C @IBAction, @IBOutlet, or @objc attributes.

> **Note** If your Swift interface references any Objective-C APIs from other files, those Objective-C interfaces will not be listed in the generated header file. You'll need to import those separately into your Objective-C files.

Now you can use the Swift APIs in your Objective-C files.

```
#import "MyModule-Swift.h"

SwiftClass *swiftClass = [[SwiftClass alloc] init]
```

Importing Objective-C into Swift in the Same Framework Target

When you create a new framework, Xcode will create an umbrella header file for your framework called <FrameworkName>.h, which replaces the bridging header for an application target.

Make sure the framework builds as a module. To do this, under the Build Settings, check that Defines Module (DEFINES_MODULE) is set to Yes.

Now import all the header files you need to expose to Swift. These header files will be available to all the Swift files in the framework, and they'll also be available when you import this framework into Swift using import Framework in a Swift file.

```
#import <MyClass1.h>
#import <MyClass2.h>
```

Importing Swift into Objective-C in the Same Framework Target

In the same way as when an application is the target, Xcode will generate an umbrella header file that Objective-C can import in order to use Swift interfaces when the target is a framework. Since this header file is part of the public interface, only the APIs marked with the public attribute are listed.

You can still use the APIs marked as internal in classes that inherit from Objective-C classes. But they are available only to Objective-C classes in the same framework; they will not be available outside the framework.

You simply import the generated header in the Objective-C files in the same framework.

```
#import <MyFramework/MyFramework-Swift.h>
```

Importing Frameworks

The process of importing frameworks written in either the same language or mixed languages is the same. The only requirement is that the framework be marked as **Defines Module** in the settings for the framework.

In Objective-C you use the @import statement, for example, @import MyFramework. Even if the framework is purely Objective-C and defines the module, you can still use it. You can replace your #import <UIKit/UIKit.h> statements with @import UIKit.

The process is the same for Swift, but use the import MyFramework statement instead.

Using Swift in Objective-C

Because Swift is a new language, it has lot of functionality that Objective-C doesn't or can't support. Thus there are some limitations as to what can be imported and used in Objective-C.

Any Swift classes or protocols must be marked with the @objc keyword before they can be used. If a Swift class is a subclass of an existing Objective-C class, the compiler will automatically add this keyword to the class. Here's a list of items defined in Swift that can't be imported into Objective-C:

- Generics
- Tuples
- Enumerations
- Structures
- Typealiases
- Global functions
- Top-level functions
- Curried functions
- Nested types
- Variadics

Once the Swift APIs have been imported into Objective-C, you can use them as you would native types.

Summary

Now you know you can use both Swift and Objective-C in your projects. Xcode makes the process quite easy, though there are caveats. Be sure to watch out for:

- Name collisions
- Marking frameworks as modules
- Correctly setting the path for bridging header
- Correctly marking interfaces with access permissions
- Frameworks exposing only interfaces with `public` access permissions

Chapter 20

Working with Core Data

Core Data is a framework that allows you to maintain an ordered data store for either in-memory or permanent storage. It is akin to a database, but it's not a database in a traditional sense, it's not a relational database management system (RDBMS). Core Data can use a traditional database as a lower layer for external storage; SQLite is one of the storage mechanisms it supports.

Core Data is an object graph and persistence store framework that provides a high-level data model via entities and the relationships among those entities. It also provides fetch requests to retrieve data that meets certain criteria. Developers use Xcode's entity editor to define the object models and relationships.

Core Data is a small framework with only few classes, but it provides quite a bit of functionality, and it takes some getting used to. Some of its features include:

- Support for key value observation (KVO) and key value coding (KVC)
- Schema migration
- Relationship maintenance
- Undo support
- Change propagation
- Filtering
- Complex queries

Here's the basic life cycle of the Core Data stack:

- Set up the stack.
- Modify the objects if needed.
- Save the objects if needed.
- Tear down the stack.

Now that you have some idea of what Core Data can do, let's take a look at the classes provided by the framework and how they fit in the life cycle of the application.

NSManagedObjectContext

NSManagedObjectContext is a temporary area where the existing objects from a backing store get brought in and modified, or where you can create new objects. If you don't save the context explicitly, these changes are not saved between the application restarts. You can think of this as a scratch pad.(On iOS this means explicitly killing an app, not just going to background mode).

NSManagedObject

Any object (entity) you define that needs to work with the Core Data stack must be a subclass of NSManagedObject. These objects live in the context until they are saved to the backing store.

NSManagedObjectModel

NSManagedObjectModel defines the schema for your entities. This is where you specify the properties of your entities and the kinds of relationships they will have with other entities. The combination of entities and relationships is the object graph. You'll be interfacing with an instance of this object.

NSPersistentStoreCoordinator

NSPersistentStoreCoordinator is the go-between for the backing store (memory or disk) and the ManagedObjectContext. When you need to load or save objects from the store, this object will do that for you.

NSFetchRequest

NSFetchRequest lets you define how you'd like to load your data from the store. You can define criteria such as the entity name (one of subclass of NSManagedObject); the sort order (how you want your objects sorted, if at all); and a predicate (how to match the objects you want).

NSPredicate

NSPredicate defines how to match objects when searching for them in external storage. This could be the name of a person, for example, and it's evaluated against each object that's read. If it evaluates to true, the object is loaded.

Creating An Application

With some background on how Core Data works in hand, it's time to start building an an iOS application. Start Xcode if it's not already started. To create a new project, select iOS ➤ Application ➤ Master-Detail Application (Figure 20-1) and call it Car Collection (Figure 20-2). Make sure to select the Use Core Data option in the project creation workflow.

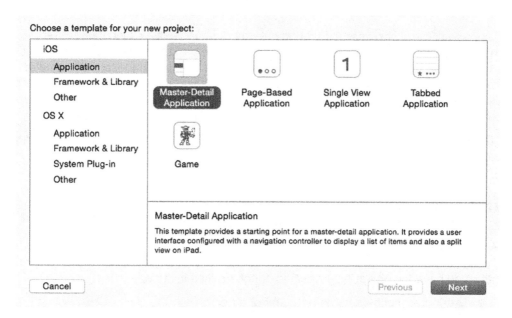

Figure 20-1. Application Template

Figure 20-2. Projects Creation Details

When the project is created, take a look at the AppDelegate.swift file. Along with the standard UIApplication delegate methods, you'll see a section for the Core Data stack with some properties already created, such as persistentStoreCoordinator, managedObjectModel, and managedObjectContext.

The managedObjectModel function will load the description of the objects you'll be defining for your project. The project template already created the Car_Collection.momd file for you (it's actually a directory but you don't need to worry about that for now).

The persistentStoreCoordinator function creates a database file called Car_Collection.sqlite, which is where you'll be saving your data. There are different options, such as an in-memory store, or XML, but for now let's stick with an SQLite database. The name of the file is based on the template but you can change it if you like. One of the items that's required is the ManagedObjectModel instance. This allows the persistantStoreCoordinator to correctly story entities the backing store.

And, finally, the managedObjectContext is where you'll be adding new objects and saving to the database.

Defining Data Objects

One of the other files is Car_Collection.xcdatamodeld, which is where you define the properties and entities you'll be using (Figure 20-3). Select the data model file. In the editor, you'll see types of objects, such as entities and fetch requests, on the left. Once you select an entity, you have the object type-specific editor. Entities include:

- Attributes, such as name or height of a person.
- Relationships to other entities; there are many types of relationships:
  - One-to-one, where an object references one other object; for example, one person having one spouse.
  - One-to-many, where an object references many other objects; for example, one parent having many children.
  - Many-to-many, where any number of objects can reference many other objects, and the reverse; for example, siblings having other siblings.
- Fetched properties, which are similar to relationships, but with these differences:
  - Values are calculated using a fetch request.
  - Fetched properties can be ordered, so they are stored in arrays instead of sets.
  - Fetched properties are evaluated lazily and the results are cached.

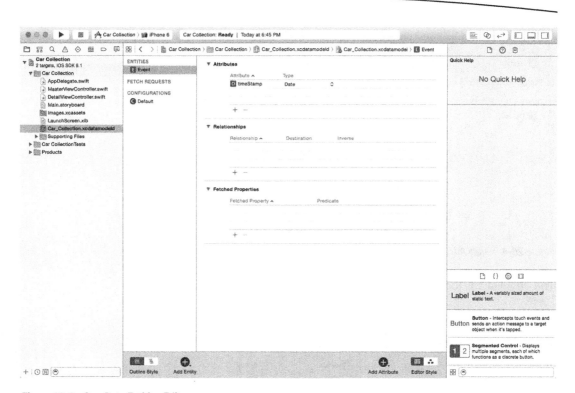

Figure 20-3. *CoreData Entities Editor*

There's a default entity called Event that you don't really need, so delete it. Now let's create the Car entity and add some attributes to it. Select the Add Entity button on the bottom of the editor. A new entity named Entity will be added to the entity list. Rename that to Car and add the attributes listed in Table 20-1.

Table 20-1. *Attributes to be added to new entity*

Attribute Name	Attribute Type
make	String
model	String
year	Date
color	String
doors	Integer 16

Under the Attributes section, select the + button to add new attributes. After adding each attribute, set its name and the type. You select the type by choosing from the pop-up menu (Figure 20-4).

Figure 20-4. *Entity Attribute Type Selection*

The final list will look like Figure 20-5.

ENTITIES

Attribute ∧	Type	
S color	String	⌄
N doors	Integer 16	⌄
S make	String	⌄
S model	String	⌄
D year	Date	⌄

Figure 20-5. *Car Entity Attributes*

If you'd like to add more properties, you can do that whenever you like. We are going to work with these for now.

The next step is to tell the controller what kind of objects to load and show. From the project navigator, look at the MasterViewController.swift file. Most of the code in this file is boilerplate that's needed by the `tableView` to show the objects. You will be modifying the `NSFetchResultsController`, the object that creates the fetch request and asks the `managedObjectContext` to load the objects based on the criteria you've set.

Look for the implementation for variable fetchedResultsController, specifically the NSEntityDescription which tells the fetchedController what kind of entity to look for. Currently it is looking for the default entity, you need to rename the entity currently called "Event". Change that to Car, and the line will look like this:

```
let entity = NSEntityDescription.entityForName("Car", inManagedObjectContext:
self.managedObjectContext!)
```

The next line to modify is the NSSortDescriptor key, which is the sort descriptor. This is where you tell how to sort the objects for displaying. Currently the sort is dependent on the `timeStamp` attribute, but you don't have to use that. In this case you should sort by the name of the car, so change it to use the `model` attribute:

```
let sortDescriptor = NSSortDescriptor(key: "model", ascending: false)
```

Now that fetching is corrected, let's correct the configuration of the cell. The implementation displays the `timeStamp` attribute, so let's change that as well. In the function `configureCell`, change it to use `model`

```
cell.textLabel!.text = object.valueForKey("model") as? String
```

The reason you need to cast this as `String` is that `valueForKey` will return an object of `AnyObject` (or in Objective-C, `id`) and the label only takes a String type. And you know that model is of string type, so you can just cast it.

If you build and run now, you'll see nothing but an empty list, with edit and add buttons. That's good. What we did was create the car collection database on external storage and load the empty data set, with correct layout for our Car entity.

The next thing to do is add a new object. Select the add button. Oops! That crashed the application! Let's look at the reason. Here's the error message:

```
2015-02-07 20:26:54.924 Car Collection[16383:2800553] *** Terminating app due to
uncaught exception 'NSUnknownKeyException', reason: '[<NSManagedObject 0x7f9033a0d570>
setValue:forUndefinedKey:]: the entity Car is not key value coding-compliant for the key
"timeStamp".'
```

This indicates that you tried to add a new Car and to set the `timeStamp` attribute, but `Car` doesn't have that attribute. Go back to the MasterViewController.swift file and look at the `insertNewObject` function. It's a simple method that creates a new object in the context and adds the `timeStamp` of when it was created. However, the `Car` object needs more attributes, so you'll have to create a new view to edit the properties.

Adding an Object Editor

Go to the Main.storyboard file to add a new view controller that will let you edit the attributes for your `Car`. Start by adding a new view controller to the project by selecting File ➤ New ➤ File… and selecting Cocoa Touch Class (Figure 20-6).

Figure 20-6. *Creating new Controller*

Then name the new controller as shown in Figure 20-7.

Figure 20-7. *Naming the New Controller*

Select the View Controller object from the object palette (Figure 20-8) and drag it to the storyboard.

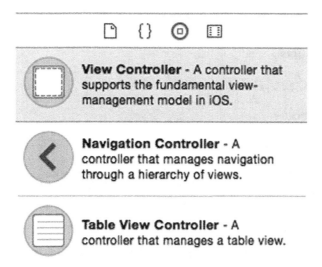

Figure 20-8. Object Template Pane

When you have the controller in the storyboard, select the view controller and then select the identity inspector. Then change the custom class to the new view controller, and add the storyboard identifier (Figure 20-9).

Figure 20-9. Controller Details Editor

Now you'll embed this view controller in a navigation controller. Select the view controller in the storyboard, then go to the editor menu and select Embed In Item and then Navigation Controller under the submenu. Once you have a new navigation controller, set the storyboard identifier for the new navigation controller to be "editorNavigationController". You'll be instantiating the view controller with this name.

Now you need to add a few more items to your view controller. Add four text fields, Make, Model, Color, and Doors and set the placeholder for the text fields in order to prompt the user to enter those values (Figure 20-10).

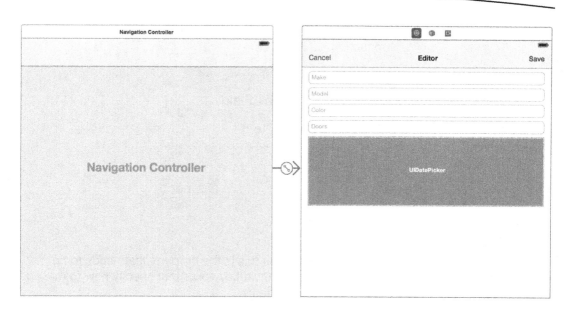

Figure 20-10. Editor Controller with Navigation Controller

Then add a date-picker object where you can set the year for the car. Also add Save and Cancel buttons so you can either save or dismiss the view controller depending on whether you want to save or cancel the new Car.

Next you need to add code to populate the view with your data if you have an existing object, or you need to create a new one. Connect each of these items to your controller outlets. Select the view controller and open the assistant editor.

Select each item and then press the control key and drag to the source file (this is called control-drag). This will create outlets for each item. You should now have five outlets with appropriate names.

Once you control-drag to your source file, the editor will ask you to name each outlet. The editor will prefill most of the defaults for the outlet that make sense. All you have to do is enter the name of the outlet (Figure 20-11).

Figure 20-11. Adding Outlet

The first @IBOutlet keyword tells the compiler that this is the property that needs to be created from the storyboard. This is followed by Swift keywords that specify how to manage memory and the name and type of the interface items.

In the editor, you'll see a small circle left of the line numbers (Figure 20-12). This indicates that the outlet has been connected to an object in the storyboard.

```
13
14    @IBOutlet weak var makeTextField: UITextField!
15    @IBOutlet weak var modelTextField: UITextField!
16    @IBOutlet weak var colorTextField: UITextField!
17    @IBOutlet weak var numberOfDoorsTextField: UITextField!
18    @IBOutlet weak var makeYearDatePicker: UIDatePicker!
19
```

Figure 20-12. Editor Outlets

Add another property called managedObjectContext, which you'll set when you show this view controller.

```
var managedObjectContext: NSManagedObjectContext? = nil
```

Make sure to add the import Core Data statement at the top of the file. This will ensure you have the Core Data module available in this file.

Now you need to connect the Save and Cancel buttons so they can perform some actions for you. This time when you control-drag the Cancel button, you need to change the type of connection in the pop-up to Action instead of Outlet, and make the name "cancel" (Figure 20-13).

Figure 20-13. Adding an Action

And after setting the attributes and selecting Connect, the editor will add an action function that will be called when you select the Cancel button. The function is just like other instance functions except with the @IBAction keyword before the func keyword to let the compiler know that this function will be called from an object in the storyboard.

```
@IBAction func cancel(sender: UIBarButtonItem) {
}
```

This is an empty function so add some code to dismiss the view controller:

```
@IBAction func cancel(sender: UIBarButtonItem) {
self.presentingViewController?.dismissViewControllerAnimated(true, completion: nil)
}
```

Now do the same with the Save button. First, name the function save.

```
@IBAction func save(sender: UIBarButtonItem) {
}
```

Then fill in code for the save function:

```
@IBAction func save(sender: UIBarButtonItem) {
    let context = self.managedObjectContext
    let entityName = "Car"
    let newManagedObject = NSEntityDescription.insertNewObjectForEntityForName(entityName,
    inManagedObjectContext: context!) as NSManagedObject

    newManagedObject.setValue(self.makeTextField.text ?? "Unknown Make", forKey: "make")
    newManagedObject.setValue(self.modelTextField.text ?? "Unknown Model", forKey: "model")
    newManagedObject.setValue(self.colorTextField.text ?? "Unknown Color", forKey: "color")
    let doors : NSString = self.numberOfDoorsTextField.text ?? "2"
    let number = NSNumber(int: doors.intValue)
```

```
newManagedObject.setValue(number, forKey: "doors")
newManagedObject.setValue(self.makeYearDatePicker.date, forKey: "year")

var error: NSError? = nil
if !context!.save(&error) {
}

self.presentingViewController?.dismissViewControllerAnimated(true, completion: nil)
}
```

The first line creates a local reference to the context and the second sets the name of the entity to create.

The next line actually creates an entity of type `Car` and inserts it into the `managedObjectContext`. If you don't set any attributes, the entity would still exist. But let's add some.

The next three lines take the values from the text fields and add those to the new entity. The line after that is a bit tricky because you're setting the type of the doors to integer. You have to store the integer as an `NSNumber` because Core Data stores objects, not primitives. And, lastly, the code just takes the date and adds the year.

After setting the attributes, save your object to storage by calling the `save` instance method on the `managedObjectContext`.

Finally, dismiss the controller, and go back to the list of cars.

Showing the Editor

Now that you have an editor, how do you show it? Remember that you have an `insertNewObject` in the `MasterViewController`. You're going to remove the existing code and replace it with the following code to instantiate the navigation controller and present it.

```
func insertNewObject(sender: AnyObject) {
        let navController = self.storyboard?.instantiateViewControllerWithIdentifier
        ("editorNavigationController") as? UINavigationController
        let editorViewController = navController?.topViewController as
        DetailEditorViewController
        editorViewController.managedObjectContext = self.managedObjectContext;
        self.navigationController?.presentViewController(navController!, animated: true,
        completion: nil);
}
```

This function will instantiate the navigation controller you added, along with its root view controller, which is the editor controller. Get your editor controller and then set the `managedObjectContext` since you want to create objects in this context, and then present it on the screen.

Now experiment with this and add some cars. Once you add a car and dismiss the editor by saving, you'll see that car immediately show up in your list.

Entity Classes

You probably noticed that you didn't actually create an entity class called Car and that we have used the setValue:forKey: method on NSManagedObject to set the attributes, which doesn't seem elegant. Let's fix that by creating a class for the Car object and then use it to simply add the attributes directly.

Start by selecting File ➤ New ➤ File… and then choosing Core Data from the left pane and the NSManagedObject subclass on the right (Figure 20-14). Then press Next and you will see the screen in Figure 20-15.

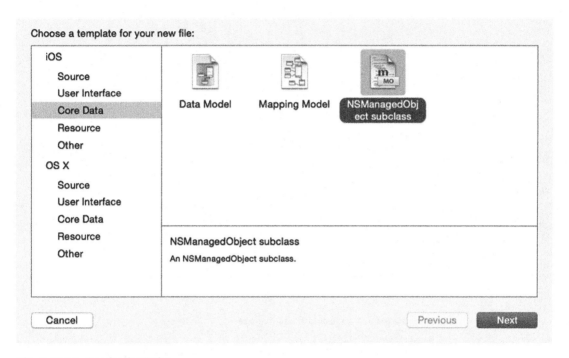

Figure 20-14. Creating Car Entity

Choose a template for your new file:

Select the data models with entities you would like to manage

Select	Data Model
☑	Car_Collection

Cancel   Previous   Next

Figure 20-15. *Selecting the Object Model*

Since you only have one object model, it's already selected and you simply go to the next screen shown in Figure 20-16.

Choose a template for your new file:

Select the entities you would like to manage

Select	Entity
☑	Car

Cancel   Previous   Next

Figure 20-16. *Selecting the Entity*

If you have more than one entity, they will be listed and you can select the entities you want to create the classes for. Press Next and save the files. From the file creation dialog, make sure to select options as shown in Figure 20-17.

Figure 20-17. *File Creation Options*

Now you have a class called `Car`:

```swift
class Car: NSManagedObject {
    @NSManaged var color: String
    @NSManaged var doors: NSNumber
    @NSManaged var make: String
    @NSManaged var model: String
    @NSManaged var year: NSDate
}
```

The properties are marked with @NSManaged, which tells Swift that these properties need special treatment when they're accessed. If you try build and run, you'll get a warning from Core Data that it can't find the class for the entity:

```
2015-02-07 22:26:06.394 Car Collection[17018:3500332] CoreData: warning: Unable to load
class named 'Car' for entity 'Car'.  Class not found, using default NSManagedObject instead.
```

What's happening here? Well, remember that Swift uses namespaces. The actual name of the class is `Car_Collection.Car`, which is indeed not the class `Car` Core Data is looking for. As you learned in Chapter 18, you have to give this class an Objective-C name that Core Data can understand. Just add `@objc(Car)` before the `class` keyword. Now update the rest of the methods to use this new class.

The save method in the editor view controller now looks much better:

```
@IBAction func save(sender: UIBarButtonItem) {
    let context = self.managedObjectContext
    let entityName = "Car"
    let newCar = NSEntityDescription.insertNewObjectForEntityForName(entityName,
    inManagedObjectContext: context!) as Car
    newCar.make = self.makeTextField.text ?? "Unknown Make"
    newCar.model = self.modelTextField.text ?? "Unknown Model"
    newCar.color = self.colorTextField.text ?? "Unknown Color"
    let doors : NSString = self.numberOfDoorsTextField.text ?? "2"
    let number = NSNumber(int: doors.intValue)
    newCar.doors = number
    newCar.year = self.makeYearDatePicker.date

    var error: NSError? = nil
    if !context!.save(&error) {
    }

    self.presentingViewController?.dismissViewControllerAnimated(true, completion: nil)
}
```

Now update the `MasterViewController` to use this new class to configure the cell.

```
func configureCell(cell: UITableViewCell, atIndexPath indexPath: NSIndexPath) {
    let car = self.fetchedResultsController.objectAtIndexPath(indexPath) as Car
    cell.textLabel!.text = car.model
}
```

Now you can use the properties of the entity directly instead of using the `objectForKey`, and casting the correct type.

Summary

Core Data is a small framework but requires some time and effort to learn and to understand its idiosyncrasies. Many books have been written on the subject. One such book is *Pro Core Data for iOS* (Apress, 2011). This chapter is just a taste of what Core Data can and can't do. You have to look at the life cycle of objects and different parts of the systems and see what roles they play. There are many libraries that make working with Core Data much easier and handle most of the boilerplate code.

Chapter 21

Consuming RESTful Services

If you have a Twitter account or a Facebook account, when you use their mobile applications you are consuming their services via a REST API.

Representational State Transfer (REST) defines an architecture, not a protocol, for designing Web services that consume system resources. It defines how the resource states are accessed and transferred over HTTP.

The key features of REST Web services are:

- They use HTTP methods only.
- They are stateless.
- Endpoints are defined as directory structures.
- Data is transferred using XML, JSON or both.

HTTP Methods

There are four HTTP methods, GET, PUT, POST and DELETE. These methods are defined by the HTTP protocol.

- GET is used to retrieve a resource from the server.
- POST is used to create a resource on the server.
- PUT is used to modify an existing resource on the server.
- DELETE is used to remove a resource from the server.

It's not good design to use specific methods for the purpose of other methods. For instance, it's not a good idea to use GET to create a resource on the server.

Being Stateless

Since REST services need to scale and serve lots of requests, it's difficult to keep track of each connection between multiple requests from the same client. This is especially true in an environment where the backend may use load balancers, proxies, or failovers. So every call must be completely independent of every other call, and must send all the information needed to complete the request.

Endpoints

Each endpoint must be defined as a path to a resource; resources are also known as URIs. When designing the endpoints, make sure they are well thought out and extensible. Here are some examples:

```
GET http://www.mydomain.com/v1/user/<userId>
GET http://www.mydomain.com/v1/forum/rooms
GET http://www.mydomain.com/v1/forum/topic/<topidId>
POST http://www.mydomain.com/v1/forum/topic/<topicId>
```

Data Formats

When sending the retrieving resource, it can be packaged in a structured format that the server and client know how to interpret. The officially recommended formats are either XML (eXtensible Markup Language) or JSON (JavaScript Object Notation). Apple provides built-in APIs to decode and encode into these formats. Depending on which format you end up using, make sure to set the correct HTTP headers to indicate what kind of data it is.

MIME type	Content Type
JSON	application/json
XML	application/xml

Network Access

iOS and OSX provide an extensive set of APIs to handle these requests. Some of the APIs you'll be using are:

- NSURL and NSURLComponents, which allow you to create the URIs for the endpoints.

- NSURLRequest, along with URL and other information, makes a complete request needed to interact with sever

- NSURLSession is the actual object that uses the request to download and upload the resource

- NSJSONSerialization encodes and decodes JSON objects for transfer

- NSXMLParser decodes XML data

Now that you have most of the pieces, it's time to create the application to put the pieces together. There are many APIs to choose from for your REST application. I'm going to work with the Hacker News API.

> **Note** Hacker News is social news site that has stories related to programmers. You'll find the official API at `https://github.com/HackerNews/API`.

My application will download the top stories and display them in a table view. First let's take a look at the API. The base URL for the app to make calls to the API is:

`https://hacker-news.firebaseio.com/v0/`

And some of the endpoints I'm interested in are:

`/topstories.json` returns the current set of top stories on the front page, returning the identifiers for the stories as an array.

`[identifier1, identifier2, ... ]`

`/item/<itemnumber>.json` returns the detail information about one of the stories. You specify the story identifier you need more information about, such as `/item/<identifier>.json` and the typical result will be returned as key-value pairs (that is, a dictionary), as shown in Table 21-1.

Table 21-1. Key-value pairs

Key	Value
id	Unique identifier for the item
by	User who posted the item
type	One of job, story, comment, poll, or pollopt
time	Time item was created on the system
title	Title of the item
url	URL of the item, if any
score	Current score of the item
kids	An array of comment identifiers

There are a few others, but I'll focus on these for now. Let's create a new project and call it News. I'm going to use project template called Master-Detail Application, as shown in Figure 21-1.

Choose a template for your new project:

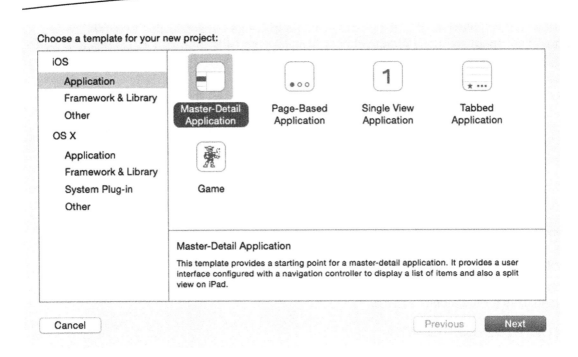

Figure 21-1. *Choosing the Master-Detail Application template*

First I need to create a class that represents an item, so I'll create a new Swift file using the Swift file template from the new file panel. The file is called `Item.swift` and it defines some properties and a method to update the properties:

```
public class Item {
    let identifier : Int

    init(dictionary : [String : AnyObject]) {
        let identifier = dictionary["id"] as NSNumber
        self.identifier = Int(identifier.intValue)
        self.score = 0
        self.update(dictionary)
    }

    var type : String? = nil
    var by : String? = nil
    var date : NSDate? = nil
    var title : String? = nil
    var url : NSURL? = nil
    var score : Int32
    var text : String? = nil

    public func update(dictionary : [String : AnyObject]) {
        self.type = dictionary["type"] as? String
        self.by = dictionary["by"] as? String
```

```
    let unixTime = dictionary["time"] as? NSNumber
    if let time : NSNumber = unixTime {
        self.date = NSDate(timeIntervalSince1970 : time.doubleValue) as NSDate
    }
    self.title = dictionary["title"] as? String

    let urlString = dictionary["url"] as? String
    if let string = urlString {
        self.url = NSURL(string: string)
    }
    let score = dictionary["score"] as? NSNumber

    if let value : NSNumber = score {
        self.score = Int32(value.intValue)
    }
    self.text = dictionary["text"] as? String
    }
}
```

Next I need to connect to the service and download items. I'll download the identifiers for the top stories and then, for each of these stories, I'll download the details.

In the `MasterViewController` I'll create a couple of functions that will download the items I need.

```
private func  getTopStories() -> Void {
    let url = NSURL(string: NetworkManagerBaseURL + "/v0/topstories.json")
    var urlRequest = NSMutableURLRequest(URL: url!)
    urlRequest.HTTPMethod = "GET"
    NSURLConnection.sendAsynchronousRequest(urlRequest, queue: self.operationQueue)
    {[unowned self] (response, responseData, error) -> Void in
        if let data = responseData {

    let objects = NSJSONSerialization.JSONObjectWithData(data, options:
    NSJSONReadingOptions(0), error: nil) as? NSArray

            self.downloadStoriesInformation(objects!)
        }
    }
}
```

First I'll create a URL for the endpoint by creating an NSURL object. Once I have the URL object I then create a request from that URL. After I have the request object, I want to set the method I'll use for downloading. In this case I want GET.

Note   GET is the default method NSURLRequest uses if you don't change it. I'll set it to be verbose.

Next I use the `NSURLConnection` class method to download the data. This method returns an HTTP response object, and data if there is data, or an error if there was an error.

I can't use the raw `NSData` so I have to convert the data into a proper native object. I do this using `NSJSONSerialization`. After I have the top stories I need to download each story detail.

I'm going to set up the few items I'll need before starting to code. The first item is the base URL from which I'll download the news articles:

```
let NetworkManagerBaseURL = "http://hacker-news.firebaseio.com"
```

Next I need an operation queue where I'll schedule the download processes.

```
var operationQueue : NSOperationQueue = {
    var operationQueue = NSOperationQueue()
    operationQueue.name = "com.apress.DownloadQueue"
    operationQueue.maxConcurrentOperationCount = 1
    return operationQueue
}()
```

The next method downloads the story details for each story, and once I have all the stories I show them in my tableview.

```
private func downloadStoriesInformation (storyIdentifiers : NSArray) -> Void {
    var downloaded : Int = 0
    let count = storyIdentifiers.count
    for var index : Int = 0; index < count; index++ {
        let storyIdentifier = storyIdentifiers[index] as NSNumber
        let urlString = NetworkManagerBaseURL + "/v0/item/" + storyIdentifier.stringValue +
        ".json"
        let url = NSURL(string: urlString)
        var urlRequest = NSMutableURLRequest(URL: url!)
        urlRequest.HTTPMethod = "GET"


NSURLConnection.sendAsynchronousRequest(urlRequest, queue: self.operationQueue)
{[unowned self] (response, responseData, error) -> Void in
            if let data = responseData {
                let object = NSJSONSerialization.JSONObjectWithData(data, options:
                NSJSONReadingOptions(0), error: nil) as? NSDictionary
                let item = Item(dictionary: object as [String : AnyObject])
                self.stories.setObject(item, forKey: storyIdentifier)
                downloaded++
                if downloaded == count {
                    self.objects.removeAllObjects()
                    self.objects.addObjectsFromArray(storyIdentifiers)
                    dispatch_async(dispatch_get_main_queue()) { [unowned self] in
                        self.tableView.reloadData()
                    }
                }
            }
        }
    }
}
```

After I have the data, I want to display it. To do this I need to modify the
cellForRow:atIndexPath: method to display the title of the story.

```
override func tableView(tableView: UITableView, cellForRowAtIndexPath indexPath:
NSIndexPath) -> UITableViewCell {
    let cell = tableView.dequeueReusableCellWithIdentifier("Cell", forIndexPath: indexPath)
    as UITableViewCell

    let object = objects[indexPath.row] as NSNumber
    let item = self.stories[object] as Item
    cell.textLabel!.text = item.title
    return cell
}
```

I have the order of the stories in my objects property, as well as the data related to how to
get the stories.

Once I have the list of stories and titles, to actually read the article I update the detail view to
show the contents of the story. The steps required are:

- Remove the existing elements from the view
- Add UIWebView as a subview to the view
- Send the new item so I can load the article.

After deleting any subview from the detail view, I'll drag the UIWebView object from the object
panel and drop it on the view.

Next I'll add the outlet named webView by control-dragging to the DetailViewController.
Then I need to set the DetailViewController as the delegate for the webView. To do this,
I control-drag from the webView to the DetailViewController. Also, I need to have the
DetailViewController conform to UIWebViewDelegate since it's the delegate for the UIWebView.
I simply add the UIWebViewController to the class definition.

```
class DetailViewController: UIViewController, UIWebViewDelegate {
```

Next I need to change the type information for detailItem from AnyObject to Item

```
var detailItem: Item? {
    didSet {
        // Update the view.
        self.configureView()
    }
}
```

In the `MasterViewController` I need to update the `prepareForSegue` function to set the correct value for the `detailItem`.

```
override func prepareForSegue(segue: UIStoryboardSegue, sender: AnyObject?) {
    if segue.identifier == "showDetail" {
        if let indexPath = self.tableView.indexPathForSelectedRow() {
            let object = objects[indexPath.row] as NSNumber
    let item = stories[object] as Item
            (segue.destinationViewController as DetailViewController).detailItem = item
        }
    }
}
```

When `DetailViewController` has the item, I need to load the web page for the story and I need to update the configure function.

```
func configureView() {
    // Update the user interface for the detail item.
    if let detail: Item = self.detailItem {
        if let view = self.webView {
            let url = detail.url
            let urlRequest = NSURLRequest(URL: url!)
            view.loadRequest(urlRequest)
        }
    }
}
```

I get the URL from the item and make a request, and then tell `webView` to load the request. Now I'll add the title for the story to be the title of the detail view. To do that I need to implement a delegate method called `webViewDidFinishLoad`. `WebView` will call this method once it has loaded the page.

```
func webViewDidFinishLoad(webView: UIWebView) {
    let title = webView.stringByEvaluatingJavaScriptFromString("document.title")
    self.title = title
}
```

Summary

This is a quick look at REST services, what they are and how you can use them to access the data from servers. This is the same method a Twitter client would use to connect to its server and download tweets. If you do a quick search on the web for REST API, you'll find many companies that offer REST APIs for their resources. If you plan on writing a client-server application for mobile, this a good solution.

Chapter 22

Developing a Swift-Based Application

Now that you've learned all about Swift, let's build an application in Swift. You'll use most of the techniques discussed in previous chapters to develop a health-related app based on Apple's HealthKit, a framework that allows you to store and share fitness and health data. And you'll take advantage of HealthKit's companion application, called Health, which can provide a quick overview of the information entered into the HealthKit database.

Health applications allow users to take data from external instruments that support the HealthKit API, such as pedometers and fitness trackers. HealthKit doesn't upload data anywhere due to the sensitive nature of health data. It is recommended that you do the same with information you read and write to the database.

> **Note**   HealthKit is supported only on iOS8 or later, and only on some devices.

The Project

One of the items people keep track of on a daily basis is their blood pressure; so let's create an application that allows a user to keep a log of his or her blood pressure data.

Here are the basic steps to develop the application:

- Create a new project.
- Enable HealthKit for your project.
- Check the availability of HealthKit support for your device.

▨ Load the HealthKit Store.

▨ Ask the user for permission to read and write data to the HealthKit Store.

▨ Add the sample to the store.

Note   Blood Pressure readings are defined as Systolic/Diastolic mm Hg:

Systolic   The top number, which measures the pressure in the arteries when the heart heart muscle contracts.

Diastolic   The bottom number, which measures the pressure in the arteries between heartbeats when the heart muscle is resting between beats and refilling with blood.

Creating a Project

You've already created a number of projects as you went through the book. Now you'll create one more, so start Xcode.

Create a new project using File ➤ New ➤ Project… and then, in the project template window, select the Master-Detail Application template as shown in Figure 22-1.

Figure 22-1. Choosing an Application Template

Name the project BPLog, make sure to select Swift and other properties as shown in Figure 22-2, then press Next to save the project.

Choose options for your new project:

Product Name:	BPLog
Organization Name:	Apress, Inc.
Organization Identifier:	com.apress
Bundle Identifier:	com.apress.BPLog
Language:	Swift
Devices:	iPhone
	☐ Use Core Data

Cancel   Previous   Next

Figure 22-2. Selecting Application Properties

Next, you need to enable HealthKit for the project. Select the project from the project navigator, and then select the application target.

Before you can enable HealthKit support, you need to choose Team in the general information pane as shown in Figure 22-3 under the Identity section. The developer center creates credentials for your application and those credentials are need to develop applictions that use HealthKit.

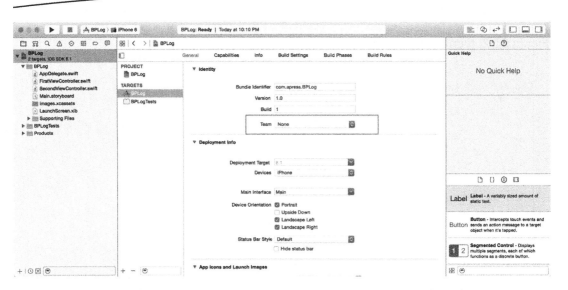

Figure 22-3. Selecting the Team

Note   If you haven't yet signed up as a developer with Apple, this is a good time to do so. You won't be able to create a HealthKit application without doing so.

After choosing the team under which the application will be developed, enable HealthKit by selecting the Capabilities tab as shown in Figure 22-4.

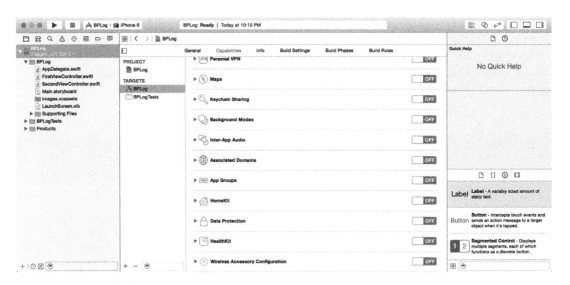

Figure 22-4. Capabilities Page

As you scroll down the list of capabilities, make sure HealthKit is turned on as shown in Figure 22-5. Once it's enabled, Xcode will generate an entitlements file and add it to your project, along with HealthKit.framework.

Figure 22-5. Enabling HealthKit for Project

After the project is set up, you need to check whether the OS of the target device supports HealthKit; even though you might be running iOS8, some devices, such as the iPad, do not support HealthKit yet.

Select the `MasterViewController`. Before you can use any of the HealthKit functionality, you need to import HealthKit, at the top of the file, right after `import UIKit`, add the `import HealthKit` statement:

```
import UIKit
import HealthKit
```

Now you're ready to work with HealthKit. To check if the health data is available, you ask the HKHealthStore, add the following line at the end of the `viewDidLoad` method.

```
let healthDataAvailable = HKHealthStore.isHealthDataAvailable()
```

This is a class method that returns if the HealthKit is supported. If HealthKit is supported, you need to ask for permission to access the health data. Before you can do that, however, you need to create an instance of `HKHealthStore`. Let's add a property called `healthStore` right below the `objects` property.

```
var healthStore : HKHealthStore ? = nil
```

This statement will create an instance of a variable where an instance of the HealthStore will be saved while working with HealthKit.

Next you need to get permissions. HealthKit defines various identifiers to use when asking for permissions. Using those identifiers shown in Table 22-1, you'll create HKQuantityType objects when requesting permissions.

Table 22-1. HealthKit defined identifiers

Identifier	Type
HKQuantityTypeIdentifierHeight	Read/Write
HKQuantityTypeIdentifierBodyMass	Read/Write
HKQuantityTypeIdentifierHeartRate	Read/Write
HKQuantityTypeIdentifierBloodPressureSystolic	Read/Write
HKQuantityTypeIdentifierBloodPressureDiastolic	Read/Write
HKCharacteristicTypeIdentifierDateOfBirth	Read
HKCharacteristicTypeIdentifierBiologicalSex	Read

Now create two functions for the properties you need to access.

```
private func readDataTypes() -> NSSet {
    let heightType = HKQuantityType.quantityTypeForIdentifier(HKQuantityTypeIdentifierHeight)
    let weightType = HKQuantityType.quantityTypeForIdentifier(HKQuantityTypeIdentifier
    BodyMass)
    let heartRateType = HKQuantityType.quantityTypeForIdentifier(HKQuantityTypeIdentifier
    HeartRate)
    let bloodPressureSystolic = HKQuantityType.quantityTypeForIdentifier
    (HKQuantityTypeIdentifierBloodPressureSystolic)
    let bloodPressureDiastolic = HKQuantityType.quantityTypeForIdentifier
    (HKQuantityTypeIdentifierBloodPressureDiastolic)
    let birthDayType = HKCharacteristicType.characteristicTypeForIdentifier
    (HKCharacteristicTypeIdentifierDateOfBirth)
    let biologicalSexType = HKCharacteristicType.characteristicTypeForIdentifier
    (HKCharacteristicTypeIdentifierBiologicalSex);
    return NSSet(objects: heightType, weightType, heartRateType, bloodPressureSystolic,
    bloodPressureDiastolic, birthDayType, biologicalSexType)
}

private func writeDataTypes() -> NSSet {
    let heightType = HKQuantityType.quantityTypeForIdentifier(HKQuantityTypeIdentifierHeight)
    let weightType = HKQuantityType.quantityTypeForIdentifier(HKQuantityTypeIdentifier
    BodyMass)
    let heartRateType = HKQuantityType.quantityTypeForIdentifier(HKQuantityTypeIdentifier
    HeartRate)
    let bloodPressureSystolic = HKQuantityType.quantityTypeForIdentifier
    (HKQuantityTypeIdentifierBloodPressureSystolic)
    let bloodPressureDiastolic = HKQuantityType.
    quantityTypeForIdentifier(HKQuantityTypeIdentifierBloodPressureDiastolic)
    return NSSet(objects: heightType, weightType, heartRateType, bloodPressureSystolic,
    bloodPressureDiastolic)
}
```

Next, you need to ask for the permissions so you'll call this function from `viewDidLoad`.

```
private func requestAuthorizationAndLoadData() {
    self.healthStore = HKHealthStore()
    let readDataTypes = self.readDataTypes()
    let writeDataTypes = self.writeDataTypes()
    self.healthStore?.requestAuthorizationToShareTypes(writeDataTypes, readTypes:
    readDataTypes, completion: { [unowned self] (success, error) -> Void in
        if success {
            dispatch_async(dispatch_get_main_queue(), { () -> Void in
                self.loadData()
            })
        } else {
            println("You did not allow health store access")
        }
    })
}
```

This function gets the read and write permission type and then requests authorization. Users of the application have the choice to grant permission for each type you asked for, but you may not get all the permissions you requested.

Let's add a dummy function called `loadData` that we'll complete a bit later.

```
private func loadData() {

}
```

Also, update the `viewDidLoad` method by calling the new authorization method, adding the following code at the end of the function:

```
let healthDataAvailable = HKHealthStore.isHealthDataAvailable()
if healthDataAvailable {
    self.requestAuthorizationAndLoadData()
}
```

Build and run the application on a device that supports HealthKit. If everything goes well, you'll be asked for the permissions with the prompt shown in Figure 22-6.

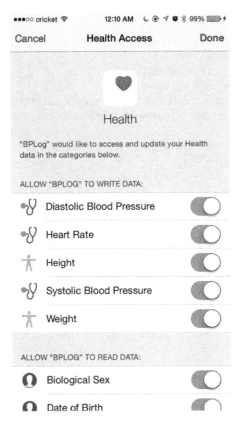

Figure 22-6. *HealthKit Permission Controller*

You can scroll down to see the rest of the permissions. These are the permissions we we requested. The top section is where you enable or diable the write permisions. The Bottom section is the read only. The reason they are different is because there are some applications you just want them to write the data, not read the data. You could write an application that only reads the data and displays in view that suits better. Here, we will allow all the permissions we asked for. If we were to deny these permissions we would not be able read and write to health store. Next, you need to get the data from the store and display it.

Before loading the data, you need to create a class where the retrieved data will be stored. The data will be returned as a key value store or a dictionary. It would be good to just make an object to represent the blood pressure item. Start by creating a new Swift file using File ➤ New ➤ File.... Select iOS ➤ Source ➤ Swift File as shown in Figure 22-7.

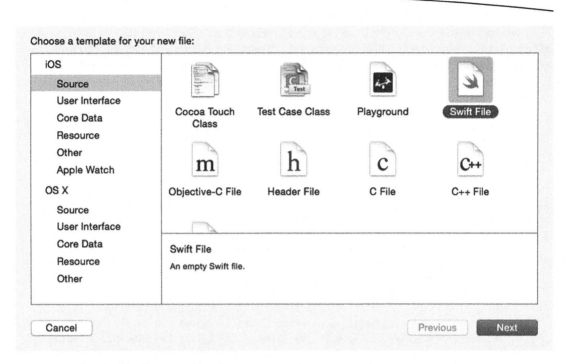

Figure 22-7. Creating BloodPressure object file

Name the file BloodPressureItem and add it to the project. Now select the newly created file
BloodPressureItem.swift. You're going to create a new class with the same name as the file
and add four properties: pressureSystolic, pressureDiastolic, startDate, and endDate.

You'll also create an init method to initialize the item with the values for blood pressure.
The class will look like this:

```
import Foundation

class BloodPressureItem {
    private (set) var pressureSystolic : Double = 0.0
    private (set) var pressureDiastolic : Double = 0.0
    var startDate : NSDate = NSDate ()
    var endDate : NSDate = NSDate()

    required init(systolic : Double, pressureDiastolic diastolic : Double) {
        self.pressureSystolic = systolic
        self.pressureDiastolic = diastolic
    }
}
```

Notice that we created the setters for blood pressure types to be private, to force creation
using the init method with values so we can validate before creating the item.

Next we create an extension to the `BloodPressureItem` that will convert to and from `HKCorrelation`, because HealthKit returns the correlation objects with values. You can add the extension in the MasterViewController but I think it makes sense to add it in the `BloodPressureItem`.

> **Note**   These functions don't need to be in an extension. You can have them as part of the class definition if you like.

```
extension BloodPressureItem {
    convenience init(correlation : HKCorrelation) {
        let bloodPressureUnit: HKUnit = HKUnit.millimeterOfMercuryUnit()
        let bloodPressureSystolicType = HKQuantityType.
        quantityTypeForIdentifier(HKQuantityTypeIdentifierBloodPressureSystolic)
        let bloodPressureDiastolicType = HKQuantityType.
        quantityTypeForIdentifier(HKQuantityTypeIdentifierBloodPressureDiastolic)
        let systolicSet = correlation.objectsForType(bloodPressureSystolicType) as NSSet
        let diastolicSet = correlation.objectsForType(bloodPressureDiastolicType) as NSSet
        let bloodPressureSystolicSample = systolicSet.anyObject() as HKQuantitySample
        let bloodPressureDiastolicSample = diastolicSet.anyObject() as HKQuantitySample
        let systolicQuantity = bloodPressureSystolicSample.quantity
        let diastolicQuantity = bloodPressureDiastolicSample.quantity
        let systolic = systolicQuantity.doubleValueForUnit(bloodPressureUnit) as Double
        let diastolic = diastolicQuantity.doubleValueForUnit(bloodPressureUnit) as Double
        self.init(systolic: systolic, pressureDiastolic : diastolic)
        self.startDate = bloodPressureSystolicSample.startDate
        self.endDate = bloodPressureSystolicSample.endDate
    }

    func asCorrelation() -> HKCorrelation {
        let bloodPressureUnit: HKUnit = HKUnit.millimeterOfMercuryUnit()
        let bloodPressureSystolicQuantity: HKQuantity = HKQuantity(unit: bloodPressureUnit,
        doubleValue: self.pressureSystolic)
        let bloodPressureDiastolicQuantity: HKQuantity = HKQuantity(unit: bloodPressureUnit,
        doubleValue: self.pressureDiastolic)
        let bloodPressureSystolicType: HKQuantityType = HKQuantityType.
        quantityTypeForIdentifier(HKQuantityTypeIdentifierBloodPressureSystolic)
        let bloodPressureDiastolicType: HKQuantityType = HKQuantityType.
        quantityTypeForIdentifier(HKQuantityTypeIdentifierBloodPressureDiastolic)
        let startDate = self.startDate
        let endDate = self.endDate
        let bloodPressureSystolicSample: HKQuantitySample = HKQuantitySample(type:
        bloodPressureSystolicType, quantity: bloodPressureSystolicQuantity, startDate:
        startDate, endDate: endDate)
        let bloodPressureDiastolicSample: HKQuantitySample = HKQuantitySample(type:
        bloodPressureDiastolicType, quantity: bloodPressureDiastolicQuantity, startDate:
        startDate, endDate: endDate)
        var objects : NSSet = NSSet(objects: bloodPressureSystolicSample,
        bloodPressureDiastolicSample)
```

```
        var bloodPressureType: HKCorrelationType = HKObjectType.
        correlationTypeForIdentifier(HKCorrelationTypeIdentifierBloodPressure)
        var bloodPressureCorrelation : HKCorrelation = HKCorrelation(type:
        bloodPressureType, startDate: startDate, endDate: endDate, objects: objects)
        return bloodPressureCorrelation
    }
}
```

The first function is a convenience initializer, which takes a correlation item and creates an instance of BloodPressureItem. The other function converts the BloodPressureItem to a correlation so it can be stored in HealthStore.

Because blood pressure is stored in *millimeters of mercury (mmHg),* you need to create that unit in order to store the item correctly. HKUnit defines that for us.

The next two lines define the kind of information that's needed, in this case the systolic and diastolic values for blood pressure. Use the HKQuantityType class, which has various types already defined.

Next, query the correlation for the needed values, which are stored as Sets, even if you store just one value. Once you have the Set objects, you can just take any object, since you know there's only one value stored. These values are stored as HKQuantitySample. The object has a start and end date along with a quantity. Once you have a sample, you need to get the actual quantity, which is the HKQuantity object.

HKQuantity has the unit and the actual value for the sample. When you have the quantity, you can get the values for the blood pressure and create the object.

To create the correlation object from the BloodPressureItem, the process is the reverse.

With the pieces in place, let's fill in the loadData method. The first thing you need is the date range. It can be any length as long as the data is available. To make a date range, create a start and end date:

```
let calendar = NSCalendar.currentCalendar()
 let now = NSDate()
 let dateComponents = calendar.components(NSCalendarUnit.CalendarUnitYear |
 NSCalendarUnit.CalendarUnitMonth | NSCalendarUnit.CalendarUnitDay, fromDate:now)
 let startDate = calendar.dateFromComponents(dateComponents)

 let endDate = calendar.dateByAddingUnit(NSCalendarUnit.CalendarUnitDay, value: 1,
 toDate: startDate!, options:NSCalendarOptions(rawValue: 0))
```

In this case, let's get the data for one day. After the date range, you need to create a query to retrieve the data. First you need the type of information and in this case it's HKCorrelationTypeIdentifierBloodPressure:

```
let bloodPressure = HKCorrelationType.correlationTypeForIdentifier
(HKCorrelationTypeIdentifierBloodPressure)
let predicate = HKQuery.predicateForSamplesWithStartDate(startDate, endDate: endDate,
options: .None)
```

Next, create the actual query with the class HKSampleQuery. You have to create queries for any data that needs to be loaded from HealthKit.

```
let sampleQuery = HKSampleQuery(sampleType: bloodPressure as HKSampleType, predicate:
predicate, limit: 0, sortDescriptors: nil) { [unowned self](query, bloodPressureResults,
error) -> Void in
```

Once you have the sample query, simply execute it using executeQuery on the healthStore object.

```
self.healthStore?.executeQuery(sampleQuery)
```

In the closure for the sample query method, the samples will be returned and they can be added to the table view and displayed. Here's the loadData method:

```
private func loadData() {
    let calendar = NSCalendar.currentCalendar()
    let now = NSDate()
    let dateComponents = calendar.components(NSCalendarUnit.CalendarUnitYear |
    NSCalendarUnit.CalendarUnitMonth | NSCalendarUnit.CalendarUnitDay, fromDate:now)
    let startDate = calendar.dateFromComponents(dateComponents)

    let endDate = calendar.dateByAddingUnit(NSCalendarUnit.CalendarUnitDay, value: 7,
    toDate: startDate!, options:NSCalendarOptions(rawValue: 0))
    let bloodPressure = HKCorrelationType.
    correlationTypeForIdentifier(HKCorrelationTypeIdentifierBloodPressure)
    let predicate = HKQuery.predicateForSamplesWithStartDate(startDate, endDate: endDate,
    options: .None)
    let sampleQuery = HKSampleQuery(sampleType: bloodPressure as HKSampleType, predicate:
    predicate, limit: 0, sortDescriptors: nil) { [unowned self](query, bloodPressureResults,
    error) -> Void in
        if let results = bloodPressureResults {
            self.objects.removeAllObjects()
            for var index = 0; index < results.count; index++ {
                let bpitem = results[index] as HKCorrelation
                let item = BloodPressureItem(correlation: bpitem)
                self.objects.addObject(item)
            }
        }
        dispatch_async(dispatch_get_main_queue(), { () -> Void in
            self.tableView.reloadData()
        })
    }
    self.healthStore?.executeQuery(sampleQuery)
}
```

Next, to configure the cell to show the results, update the `cellForRow` function to get the item and show it.

```
override func tableView(tableView: UITableView, cellForRowAtIndexPath indexPath:
NSIndexPath) -> UITableViewCell {
    let cell = tableView.dequeueReusableCellWithIdentifier("Cell", forIndexPath: indexPath)
    as UITableViewCell
    let item = self.objects.objectAtIndex(indexPath.row) as BloodPressureItem
    cell.textLabel!.text = String("\(item.pressureSystolic)/\(item.pressureDiastolic)")
    return cell
}
```

We can get fancy with number formatters and units, but for now we just want to show the values.

Creating A Sample

It's time to create the data entry screen. To do this, you'll add a new view controller called `EntryViewController` and an associated view in the storyboard. Create a new file and add it to the project. Make sure to select the iOS ➤ Source ➤ Cocoa Touch Class as shown n Figure 22-8.

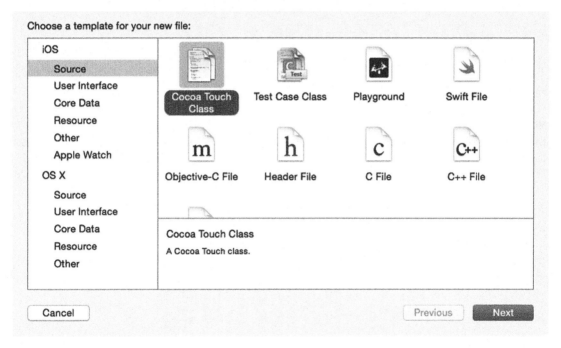

Figure 22-8. Creating a New Controller

Next, make the parent class UViewController as shown in Figure 22-9 and name it EntryViewController. Then press Next to save it.

Choose options for your new file:

Class:	EntryViewController
Subclass of:	UIViewController
	☐ Also create XIB file
	iPhone
Language:	Swift

Cancel   Previous   Next

Figure 22-9. Editing Entry View Controller Properties

Select the Main.storyboard file, drag a view controller from the object palette and add it to the storyboard. Once the view controller is added to the storyboard, set the controllers class to EntryViewController and give it a storyboard identifier.

Figure 22-10. Setting Identifier and Class for View Controller

Next, add two text fields for entry and two buttons to save and cancel the view controller as shown in Figure 22-11.

Figure 22-11. *Adding Entry Fields and Buttons*

Note   You can embed your view controller in a navigation controller and then add the cancel and save buttons. For simplicity, we just used the view controller.

Now connect the view outlets and actions for the buttons. The entry controller will have two outlets and two actions.

```
@IBOutlet weak var systolicTextField: UITextField!
@IBOutlet weak var diastolicTextField: UITextField!

@IBAction func cancel(sender: UIButton) {
}

@IBAction func save(sender: UIButton) {
}
```

Next you need to show the view controller from the MasterViewController. There's already an add button and an insertNewObject: function. You'll modify the function to show the view controller.

```
func insertNewObject(sender: AnyObject) {
    let viewController = self.storyboard?.instantiateViewControllerWithIdentifier("entryView
    Controller") as EntryViewController
    self.navigationController?.presentViewController(viewController, animated: true,
    completion: nil)
}
```

You need to be able to dismiss the entry view controller once the values have been added, so update the cancel: and save: functions to dismiss the view controller by adding the following code to both of the functions.

```
self.presentingViewController?.dismissViewControllerAnimated(true, completion: nil)
```

Now that you can show and dismiss and enter data, you need to communicate that with MasterViewController that you want to save the data. You can do this by creating a delegate protocol and a delegate property for the EntryViewController. Define the protocol as:

```
protocol EntryViewControllerDelegate {
    func entryViewControllerDidCancel(viewController : EntryViewController)
    func entryViewControllerDidSave(viewController : EntryViewController)
}
```

Then add a property called delegate of the EntryViewControllerDelegate type.

```
var delegate : EntryViewControllerDelegate? = nil
```

Now update the save and cancel methods to tell the delegate what you want to do.

```
@IBAction func cancel(sender: UIButton) {
    self.delegate?.entryViewControllerDidCancel(self)
    self.presentingViewController?.dismissViewControllerAnimated(true, completion: nil)
}
```

```
@IBAction func save(sender: UIButton) {
    self.delegate?.entryViewControllerDidSave(self)
    self.presentingViewController?.dismissViewControllerAnimated(true, completion: nil)
}
```

Next you have to update the MasterViewController to conform to this protocol and either save the data or discard it. Select the MasterViewController file and update the class definition by adding the new protocol conformation:

```
class MasterViewController: UITableViewController, EntryViewControllerDelegate {
```

This tells the compiler that the class now conforms to this protocol, and if you don't implement the functions required by the protocol the complier will complain and will not compile your project. So add the two required methods to the controller:

```
// MARK: - EntryViewControllerDelegate
func entryViewControllerDidSave(viewController: EntryViewController) {
}

func entryViewControllerDidCancel(viewController: EntryViewController) {
}
```

Next you need to tell the entry controller that you are the delegate, so update insertNewObject: and set self as the delegate for the EntryViewController.

```
let viewController = self.storyboard?.instantiateViewControllerWithIdentifier("entryViewCont
roller") as EntryViewController
viewController.delegate = self
self.navigationController?.presentViewController(viewController, animated: true,
completion: nil)
```

The next step is saving the data. Let's add a function to the EntryViewController that will return values to be saved. We are going to use a new tuple type to return a pair of values.

```
func bloodPressureValues() -> (systolic : Double, diastolic : Double) {
    let systolicString = systolicTextField.text as NSString?
    let diastolicString = diastolicTextField.text as NSString?
    var systolic = 0.0
    var diastolic = 0.0
    if let systolicValue = systolicString {
        systolic = systolicValue.doubleValue
    }
    if let diastolicValue = diastolicString {
        diastolic = diastolicValue.doubleValue
    }
    return (systolic, diastolic)
}
```

Update the MasterViewController save function to save the values in the healthStore and add the object to list to show.

```
func entryViewControllerDidSave(viewController: EntryViewController) {
    let values = viewController.bloodPressureValues()
    let bloodPressureItem = BloodPressureItem(systolic: values.systolic, pressureDiastolic:
    values.diastolic)
    let bloodPressureCorrelation = bloodPressureItem.asCorrelation()
    self.healthStore!.saveObject(bloodPressureCorrelation, withCompletion: { [unowned self]
    (success, error) -> Void in
        if success {
            dispatch_async(dispatch_get_main_queue(), { () -> Void in
                let indexPath = NSIndexPath(forRow: self.objects.count, inSection: 0)
                self.objects.addObject(bloodPressureItem)
                self.tableView.insertRowsAtIndexPaths([indexPath], withRowAnimation:
                UITableViewRowAnimation.Automatic)
            })
        }
    })
}
```

This function will save the data to the healthStore. Once the data is saved, the in-memory objects will be updated, and tableView will show the entered items.

If the user just cancels, you don't want to save the data so just dismiss the entry view controller. If you want to do anything special, you could add code to entryViewControllerDidCancel function:

```
func entryViewControllerDidCancel(viewController: EntryViewController) {
    println("User canceled, not saving data")
}
```

Next, update the cellForRowAtIndexPath function to properly display the results in the table view:

```
override func tableView(tableView: UITableView, cellForRowAtIndexPath indexPath:
NSIndexPath) -> UITableViewCell {
    let cell = tableView.dequeueReusableCellWithIdentifier("Cell", forIndexPath: indexPath)
    as UITableViewCell
    let item = self.objects.objectAtIndex(indexPath.row) as BloodPressureItem
    cell.textLabel!.text = String("\(item.pressureSystolic)/\(item.pressureDiastolic)")
    return cell
}
```

Now run the application and add a value. You should see your value displayed in the list (Figure 22-12).

Figure 22-12. Blood Pressure Values

How do you know you've actually saved the data to healthStore? Locate the Health application and launch it. Select the Health Data tab, then select Vitals. There is quite a bit of data that can be stored in HealthKit as shown in Figure 22-13. The option.

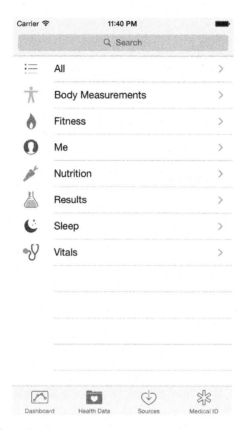

Figure 22-13. Health App Data Controller

When you do, you'll see one of the items listed is Blood Pressure as shown in Figure 22-14. Select this item.

Figure 22-14. Health app Blood Pressure Chart

You'll see the chart with data points that have been added over a period of time. Select the Show All Data option from the list. This will give you a similar list to our application. In Figure 22-15 you will see that date and which application added the values. Currently we don't have an icon for our application so a generic icon is displayed.

Figure 22-15. *Blood Pressure Values as List*

Currently, there's only one data point. If any other applications had added other data points, they'd be listed here as well. If you select the items, you can get some details as shown in Figure 22-16 . You can see that this entry was added by our application BPLog under the Source item. If you were to add a new entry from the Health app, you'd be able to see that in the application as well.

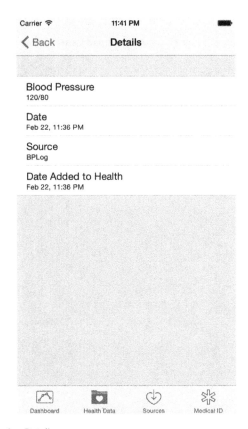

Figure 22-16. Blood Pressure value Detail

Detail View

Let's update the detail so when the user selects the items we can show the result. First you need to update the `BloodPressureItem` to have a function called `description`. This returns the values formatted as string that we can display in a label.

```
var description : NSString {
    return "\(pressureSystolic) / \(pressureDiastolic)"
}
```

You also need to update the `prepareForSegue` function to correctly set the value type.

```
override func prepareForSegue(segue: UIStoryboardSegue, sender: AnyObject?) {
    if segue.identifier == "showDetail" {
        if let indexPath = self.tableView.indexPathForSelectedRow() {
            let object = objects[indexPath.row] as BloodPressureItem
            (segue.destinationViewController as DetailViewController).detailItem = object
        }
    }
}
```

The next part to update is the `DetailViewController` to correctly look for values. Update the `detailItem` variable and `configureView` to have the correct types.

```
var detailItem: BloodPressureItem? {
    didSet {
        // Update the view.
        self.configureView()
    }
}

func configureView() {
    // Update the user interface for the detail item.
    if let detail: BloodPressureItem = self.detailItem {
        if let label = self.detailDescriptionLabel {
            label.text = detail.description
        }
    }
}
```

Now when you select the item in the list, this will trigger the detail view and show the correct values.

Summary

You have created a new application that shows the log for blood pressure, using HealthKit to save and retrieve the data. Even with such a simple application you could make use of what you learned in previous chapters. This gives you a taste of what Swift is capable of. Congratulations! You have graduated to start creating great applications of your own.

Index

Get the eBook for only $10!

Now you can take the weightless companion with you anywhere, anytime. Your purchase of this book entitles you to 3 electronic versions for only $10.

This Apress title will prove so indispensible that you'll want to carry it with you everywhere, which is why we are offering the eBook in 3 formats for only $10 if you have already purchased the print book.

Convenient and fully searchable, the PDF version enables you to easily find and copy code—or perform examples by quickly toggling between instructions and   applications. The MOBI format is ideal for your Kindle, while the ePUB can be utilized on a variety of mobile devices.

Go to www.apress.com/promo/tendollars to purchase your companion eBook.

CPSIA information can be obtained at www.ICGtesting.com
Printed in the USA
LVOW03s1019160815

450306LV00007B/119/P